D1431977

Retired
DREAMS

Paul B. Dixon

Retired
DREAMS

Dom Casmurro
Myth and Modernity

Purdue University Press
West Lafayette, Indiana

Chapter 4 appeared in an earlier version in *Discurso Literario* and is published here by permission.

Book and cover designed by H. Lind Babcock

Published in 1989

Printed in the United State of America

Library of Congress Cataloging-in-Publication Data

Dixon, Paul B., 1952-
    Retired dreams : Dom Casmurro, myth and modernity / by Paul B. Dixon
       p.   cm.
    Bibliography: p.
    Includes index.
    ISBN 0-911198-98-9
    1. Machado de Assis, 1839-1908. Dom Casmurro. 2. Machado de Assis, 1839-1908—Criticism and interpretation. I. Title.
PQ9697.M18D697 1989
869.3—dc19   88-29081
                                                       CIP

TO MY PARENTS

▼
CONTENTS

▼

ACKNOWLEDGMENTS

I would like to express my thanks to the Purdue Research Foundation for a summer grant that enabled me to do a good deal of the writing and revision for the book. I appreciate the valuable advice of my colleague Floyd Merrell and my former teacher Fred Clark, who read portions or all of the manuscript. Finally, thanks to my wife, Barbara Hart Dixon, for reading the manuscript, offering many helpful suggestions, and being a constant source of inspiration.

▼
INTRODUCTION

"Not everything is clear in life or in books." To find strong evidence for this understated aphorism, one need go no further than *Dom Casmurro*, the book in which it is contained (chap. 77), or Machado de Assis, the man who wrote it.

Joaquim Maria Machado de Assis was born in Rio de Janeiro in 1839 to a Portuguese mother and a Brazilian *mulato* father. By all accounts the family was extremely poor, and the boy's formal education never went beyond the elementary level. This combination of circumstances is normally enough to condemn a person to the lower rungs of Brazil's social ladder; neither race nor income nor education in itself is an over-whelming determinant, but the combination of the three is usually quite sufficient. In view of this social structure, Machado de Assis' life story is atypical, if not mysterious. He became involved with the printed word at an early age, first as a typesetter and proofreader, and later as a writer of columns on current events and ideas for various newspapers. He attended literary discussions at the city's best bookstore and gradually attracted the attention of some already important writers. All the while he was doing his own writing in all the

popular genres and reading voraciously. The growth of his reputation as a writer matches the rather steady growth in maturity,
polish, and brilliance of his works. With his growing reputation
came a series of important bureaucratic appointments—govern-
ment posts carrying high prestige but somewhat limited demands
in terms of time or creativity. These appointments were often
implicit subsidies for the best intellectuals, affording financial
security while allowing time for writing. He was made founding
president of the Brazilian Academy of Letters. By the time he died
in 1908, Machado de Assis had reached the pinnacle of Brazil's
intellectual establishment. His rise from a position of great dis-
advantage to one of supremacy reads almost like a Horatio Alger
story, in which pluck, responsibility, hard work, and tenacity are
always rewarded. If we can judge from his written works, however,
Machado never really accepted the idea that one can get ahead by
simply following the rules of the game. Most of his characters start
out in an economically advantaged position (although through no
particular personal merit) but are somehow "impoverished" in less
material ways. There are winners and losers among his characters, but the game they are involved in seems to be more one of
chance than of skill. An element of relativity or reciprocity is often
present: a person is but a small winner, or wins one day only to
lose the next.

Closer examination of the author's life sheds light on the
contingency of his characters' successes; his was no simple
victory either. Machado apparently stuttered and suffered from
epileptic seizures. He may well have had problems accepting
his racial identity. Some critics point to the beard and closely
cropped hair in his photographs as an attempt to hide his
African features, and others mention his preference for aristo-
cratic characters in his works as evidence of a racial or social
inferiority complex. The author's marriage (to a Portuguese
woman from a good family) is celebrated in Brazil as an
example of mutual devotion. Machado's sonnet dedicated to the
beloved Carolina on the occasion of her death is now one of the
classic poems of the Portuguese language. Yet even the success
of this marriage was tinged with the disappointment of child-
lessness. Machado's characters frequently speak of a desire for
parenthood or express their anxiety if deprived of that state.

I suspect that the author must have sensed a frustration
with his literary circumstances as well. Although he never
traveled far from Rio de Janeiro, there could hardly be a more

cosmopolitan writer. He admired great writers of all ages and nations—Homer, Virgil, Cervantes, Camões, Goethe, Sterne, Poe, Baudelaire—and his works are peppered with frequent allusions to writers from all over the Western world. In a literary sense he surely considered himself a citizen of the world, but it could hardly be said that the world returned the favor. He could not have been ignorant of his own genius and of his potential for international recognition. At the same time, he could not have been ignorant of the fact that he was condemned by destiny to write in Portuguese, a language that one of his contemporaries, the poet Olavo Bilac, aptly called the "sepulchre" of literature.

No Brazilian writer is more fascinating to biographers or would-be biographers than Machado de Assis, yet few Brazilian writers' lives are as stubbornly unknowable as his. Personal data about the author is scarce; references by the author to his private self are practically nonexistent. Machado maintained that the way to write an interesting book was to leave things out. By withholding data, he claimed, the book stimulates the imagination of the reader. The book of his life is vague indeed, and the conjectural activity that continues to surround that life is fine support for his thesis.[1]

A Masterpiece of Enigma

Machado's masterpiece, *Dom Casmurro,* is no less problematic than his life. Although the book has been translated into numerous languages, its title stubbornly resists translation, and I know of no case where it has appeared with a name other than the original. "Dom Casmurro" means something like "Sir Sourpuss," without sounding quite so trivial. The title is an affectionate nickname given to the narrator by his friends because of his reclusive, introverted, proudly opinionated nature.

Although it is a richly layered novel, addressing such questions as faith, truth, knowledge, art, religion, and politics, *Dom Casmurro* is basically a love story. The narrator, Bento Santiago (called by the diminutive Bentinho in younger years), tells how as an adolescent he fell for Capitu, the girl next door. As wiley and seductive a girl as ever there was, Capitu encourages Bentinho to love her and openly shows a corresponding interest in him. But is it actually Bentinho she finds attractive, or is it the higher social standing that he represents? Capitu is from a poorer family and is only able to live in the same neighborhood because her father drew the grand prize in a lottery. The two youths promise at an early age to marry each other. A serious impediment, however, stands in their way. Bentinho's widowed mother, Glória, has promised God that her only son will become a priest. The young lovers must somehow circumvent this promise without alienating Dona Glória. The two form a conspiracy in which Capitu reveals astounding manipulative capacities. A few years later—and not until Bentinho has had to spend some time attending the seminary—a solution is found to their predicament. Dona Glória satisfies her promise to God by sponsoring another young man in becoming a priest. Bentinho and Capitu then fulfill their own promise to marry.

After five years, including some years of anxious impatience for both husband and wife, a son is born. Ezequiel quickly develops two outstanding characteristics: his penchant for imitating people, down to their most subtle mannerisms, and his resemblance to an intimate friend of the family, Escobar. Is this resemblance simply an odd quirk of nature, reinforced by the child's imitative talent, or is there more to it than that? Bentinho refuses to give the matter much thought until Escobar suddenly dies. When he sees Capitu crying over the body at the wake, he is struck with a bitter recognition. Although he does not confront his wife for some time, he can no longer love her or her son. The time comes when it is impossible to withhold the accusation that Capitu has betrayed him, that Ezequiel is Escobar's child. Capitu refuses to confirm or deny his claims but merely acknowledges that the marriage is over. She spends the rest of her days in Switzerland. Ezequiel dies as a young man while on a scientific expedition in the Near East.

The question of Capitu's fidelity is subjected to an ambiguity compounded to the second power. The facts of the matter in themselves are equivocal. But beyond that there is the uncertainty introduced by the first-person narrator. Santiago, who shows insecurity in the marital relationship as well as an active imagination, is a classic example of the "unreliable narrator." But his unreliability makes the mystery of Capitu's loyalties and actions no less compelling. There *ought* to be an answer after all. If she is to have any correspondence with real life, then she either did commit adultery or she did not. Ezequiel, in order to have some tie with real life, must be *somebody's* son. Nearly a century after the novel's publication, readers and critics continue to debate the case. Unfortunately, no one yet has determined how to bring modern forensic technology to bear on the matter.

The plot's ambiguity affects other levels as well because the narrator's assertions about life, knowledge, God, and so on, are metaphorically derived from the account of his relationship with Capitu. The truth value of his conclusions depends upon that of his version of the marital conflict. Consequently, it is not surprising that scholars have had trouble reaching a consensus in their assessment of the novel's ideology or world view.

An Introduction to the Twentieth Century

As if by a bit of poetic justice, the novel's intrinsic uncertainty is matched by the uncertainty of its external circumstances. *Dom Casmurro* was published either in 1899 or in 1900, depending on how you look at it. Correspondence between Machado and his publisher, Garnier, establishes that production of the book was completed in December of 1899, but that it was not delivered or made public until January of 1900.[2] There was no date of publication on the first edition, so bibliographical reports have been divided between the two years ever since. Given the ambiguity of the book itself, it seems somehow appropriate that the date of its publication, and even its classification as a nineteenth- or twentieth-century novel, is questionable.

But why must it be one or the other? I propose that the work should be considered both. *Dom Casmurro* deserves to be recognized as a milestone, marking the end of one era and the beginning of another. In an incisive essay entitled "The Modern Apocalypse," Frank Kermode mentions a few important publications that occurred quite precisely at the turn of the century whose content causes them to assume a symbolic importance as "introductions" to our times:

> Naturally, this fuss about centuries can be seen to be based on the arbitrary calendar; it is known for a myth. . . . But if you want to defend the . . . mythical date, you could do very well. In 1900 Nietzsche died; Freud published *The Interpretation of Dreams;* 1900 was the date of Husserl's *Logic* and Russell's *Critical Exposition of the Philosophy of Leibniz.* With an exquisite sense of timing Planck published his quantum hypothesis in the very last days of the century, December 1900. Thus, within a few months, were published works which transformed or transvalued

> spirituality, the relation of language to knowing, and the very
> locus of human uncertainty, henceforth to be thought of not as an
> imperfection of the human apparatus but part of the nature of
> things, a condition of what we know.[3]

Had Machado de Assis somehow been more accessible to Frank
Kermode—had the arbitrary forces of destiny, for example,
made him a British novelist instead of a Brazilian one—I am
confident that Kermode would have found it quite fitting to
include *Dom Casmurro* on his list, acknowledging the novelist's role, along with Planck's, of examining "human uncertainty" as "part of the nature of things."

In spite of its relatively obscure circumstances in world literature, *Dom Casmurro* deserves to be recognized as such a
milestone—as one of the "last words" on the nineteenth-century
novel, and as a fitting introduction to the new novel of the
current century.

To explain my reasons for this claim, I wish to view the novel
within its general literary context but with a particular
perspective. As a novel about adultery, *Dom Casmurro* belongs
to a large and distinguished class of literary works. Tony
Tanner points out that while adultery has figured in literary
works of all ages, it seems to assume special importance in the
nineteenth century:

> It is such an obvious and legible phenomenon that many of
> those nineteenth-century novels that have been canonized as
> "great"—and in varying ways to varying degrees are felt to
> contain the furthest reaching fictional explorations into their
> age—center on adultery, that, with some exceptions, few have
> thought it worth trying to take the matter further. Yet the
> implications of this very obvious generalization involve the very
> nature and existence of the great bourgeois novel. . . .[4]

The reasons for the theme's propitiousness in the nineteenth
century are not hard to discover. This was an age obsessed with
morality. Could there have been a more satisfactory case study
for a generation intent on airing its moral and ethical preoccupations? Writers tending toward romanticism often empha-
sized the individual, personal dimension of the problem, as
with Hawthorne's examination of guilt, expiation, and condemnation in *The Scarlet Letter* or in Stendhal's portrayal of a
rather bewildered and compulsive personality in *Le Rouge et le
Noir (The Red and the Black)*. But even with these personal
treatments we cannot help but perceive at least an implied
critique of the society that has marginalized the stories'

protagonists. Some authors, such as Tolstoy with *Anna Karenina,* were primarily concerned with issues of right and wrong or with demonstrating the wages of sin. Increasingly, however, novelists tended to treat the domestic crisis of adultery as a symptom of a more general malaise, and the object of their moral discourse was society at large. In the case of Flaubert, for example, Madame Bovary's persistent *ennui* and obsessive spending are depictions of an entire bourgeoisie whose existence is devoid of satisfaction and morally bankrupt. We have no trouble seeing Balzac's adulterous family situations as microcosms representing entire classes of people. Occasionally, whole nations are involved, as in Fontane's *Unwiederbringlich (Beyond Recall),* in which the characters' shifting fidelities suggest the variable alliances among countries.

In *Adultery and the Novel* Tanner analyzes or at least mentions twenty-one works, a few from the late eighteenth and early twentieth centuries but most from the nineteenth century, which he considers to be the most significant examples of the "great bourgeois novel" involving adultery.[5] Significantly, two works by Machado de Assis—*Memórias póstumas de Brás Cubas (Epitaph of a Small Winner)* and *Dom Casmurro*—appear on the list. In one very important respect, *Dom Casmurro* is unlike all these other works. Each of the twenty others is unequivocal about the basic facts. In a couple of cases adultery is only "adultery in one's heart," but it is always clear that there has been at least an emotional breech of proper loyalties. In all other cases it is somehow clearly established that the physical act has taken place. This is, I think, rather remarkable because it is so far from the real life that many of these novelists were so intent on portraying. The whole question of marital faithfulness or unfaithfulness, as the terms themselves suggest, belongs more to the domain of hope, faith, conjecture, doubt, or suspicion than to the domain of knowledge. Practically speaking, people simply cannot monitor their spouses' activities (much less their feelings) during all their waking and sleeping hours. The nineteenth-century novel, however, seemed to be built upon the bedrock of its presumed knowledge. The whole moral tenor of these generations of novelists derived from the belief that they knew reality and knew what was right and wrong about it. This belief, it seems to me, is one important reason that their fictionalized adultery was clear-cut. How could one use a family crisis as a starting point for a grand ethical discourse if the "facts" of that crisis were not really accessible?

Of Tanner's list of novels, only *Dom Casmurro* leaves the question of adultery in the domain of conjecture. We do not know if Capitu was involved sexually with Escobar, or even if she was particularly attracted to him. This fact makes *Dom Casmurro* a very different type of novel. According to Albert Camus, "what distinguishes modern sensibility from classical sensibility is that the latter thrives on moral problems and the former on metaphysical problems."[6] Carlos Fuentes' discussion of the basic differences confronting nineteenth- and twentieth-century Latin American novelists seems to enlarge on the same idea:

> . . . un intelectual, en el siglo XIX, podía afectar los términos de la ecuación civilización-barbarie, del mundo del progreso contra el mundo del atraso. Vivía en un mundo épico y su respuesta era la epopeya. Pero en el siglo XX, el mismo intelectual debía luchar dentro de una sociedad mucho más compleja, interna y internacionalmente, donde no bastarían las armas y la razón y la moral. . . . Se inicia un tránsito del simplismo épico a la complejidad dialéctica, de una seguridad de las respuestas a la impugnación de las preguntas.[7]

> . . . intellectuals, in the nineteenth century, were able to realize the terms of the equation civilization-savagery, or a world of progress against a world of backwardness. They lived in an epic world and their response was the epic. But in the twentieth century the same intellectuals had to struggle in a much more complex society, both internally and internationally, in which arms, reason, and morality could no longer suffice. . . . There began a transition from epic simplism to dialectic complexity, from a sureness in the answers to the impugnation of the questions.

These statements point to one of the main factors distinguishing *Dom Casmurro* from the traditional bourgeois novel. Rather than beginning with a presumption of knowledge and proceeding to assert the moral truth, Machado's novel explores the axioms that make moral discourse possible. It seems primarily to ask questions rather than to provide answers: What is truth? Does it exist independent of the inquirer? How do we know? Where is the boundary between our faith and our knowledge? When we do not know, how should we act?

A Milestone in Latin America

Machado de Assis is the first Latin American, and surprisingly one of the first writers anywhere, to confront this new narrative world. Fuentes outlines several characteristics of this new generation of novelists which begins to flourish in Spanish America in the 1950s and which *Dom Casmurro* prefigures:

1. Mythification—a transition from documentary realism to the portrayal of reality in its affinity with universal myths. The mythic component of *Dom Casmurro* will be one of the principle subjects of this book.

2. The alliance of criticism and imagination—a transition from the pamphleteering tendency of earlier social criticism to a more subtle, creative treatment that still maintains its commitment. Recent criticism has discussed *Dom Casmurro* as a political allegory and a critique of Brazil's oligarchical society.[8] While not directing my attention to the historical dimension of that critique, I will show that the novel provides criticism of a type of thinking that figures in oppressive societies and that the author uses poetic devices to communicate that criticism.

3. Ambiguity—the abandonment of "epic simplism" in favor of forms of expression that more accurately reflect the complexity of modern life. As I have already brought out, *Dom Casmurro's* ambiguity, at the same time troubling and fascinating, has to do with a great deal of its extraordinary richness.

4. Humor and parody—the tendency to adopt the stance of unseriousness, even to make some very serious points. Numerous critics have discussed *Dom Casmurro's* humor, irony, and parody.[9] This book will show that the work's treatment of myth tends to be parodic.

5. Personalization—in the realm of characterization, the abandonment of stereotypes for more complex characters; in the domain of style, the movement away from linear, prosaic narration in order to cultivate several types of individualized, "defamiliarizing" techniques. In both realms Machado's novel is noteworthy. Anyone who has read the book can attest to the extraordinary depth in the creation of its characters. The work's digressive, self-referential, and densely figurative discourse is practically impossible to confuse with that of any of Machado's contemporaries.[10]

Fuentes' book is nominally about the Spanish American novel, but he tends to draw general conclusions about all Latin American narrative. For example, he says that in the traditional novel nature was the true Latin American protagonist;[11] that the Latin American writer was in a position of ambivalence, defending the underdogs but belonging to the elite;[12] and that the traditional Latin American novel appears as a static form within a static society.[13] Although Fuentes never discusses a single work of Brazilian literature, his tendency to extrapolate from the Spanish American to the Latin American is a common one and not entirely unwarranted. Brazil, after all, belongs to the same basic cultural tradition as the Spanish-speaking countries. Those who know Brazilian literature, however, cannot help but notice the inaccuracy of some of Fuentes' statements about "Latin American" narrative. For example, he claims that Jorge Luis Borges is the first great, fully urban Latin American narrator[14] and that with the work of authors such as Manuel Puig and Cabrera Infante the Latin American novel has learned to laugh for the first time.[15] Such statements may be true enough with regard to Spanish American literature, but they can only be true of Latin American literature if one disregards those who have written in Portuguese, most notably, Machado de Assis. I only emphasize this generalizing error on the part of Fuentes because it underlines the unique and seminal status of Machado de Assis in Latin American literature. Fuentes names as the founders of the modern Spanish American narrative Horacio Quiroga (1878–1937), Felisberto Hernández (1902–64), Macedonio Fernández (1874–1952), and Roberto Arlt (1900–1942).[16] If one wants to talk about the real foundations of modernity in *Latin American* literature, however, one must go back a full generation earlier and begin with Machado de Assis.

System-Builders and Skeptics

Returning to Fuentes' five landmarks of modernity, it is curious to note that two of the qualities—mythification and ambiguity—appear to be at odds with each other. Myth might be defined as a version of the world that asks to be believed implicitly or known without question. Mythmakers give us stories that are to be accepted as true and universally applicable, often in a psychological, ethical, or spiritual rather than a strictly realistic sense. Ambiguity, on the other hand, is a condition that challenges knowledge, invites questioning, and confounds axiomatic acceptance of information. Rather than indicating a flaw in Fuentes' assessment, these divergent tendencies point to writers' opposing attitudes with regard to modernity. Frank Kermode notes this same divergent tendency, classifying one group of modern writers as those who display "mythical thinking," who are "anti-schismatic" and engage in "literary primitivism"[17] and who are in love with "the System";[18] and another group as those who tend to be "schismatic," "clerkly," and "skeptical,"[19] who assert "the resistance of fact to fiction," and who are fond of "randomness" and opposing myth and "mess."[20] Confronted by a new world—transitory, contingent, and often confusing, some have responded with a retreat and others with an embrace.

Machado de Assis sensed this new world, and *Dom Casmurro* can be read as an attempt to come to terms with it. However, I will try to show that the book opts neither for the mythically-minded retreat nor for the embrace with the schism but in a curious way presents a stand-off between the two.

The status of the novel's narrator is the key to this impasse. Bento Santiago is a mythical thinker and a searcher for the System. As I will show, he casts his narration, with all its domesticity, in the mold of a heroic adventure with himself as the mythic hero. Through numerous rhetorical techniques, he gives the story epic dimensions, so that he comes to represent all the human race, on a quest for Truth, Meaning, Communion —a quest for a system holding the keys to the fullness of life. He is of course frustrated in this search. Normally this narrative set-up would provide excellent conditions for an ironic other voice, often referred to as that of the "implied author."[21] This more reliable voice, resting between the lines of the narrator's utterances, would provide a critique of the pseudo-author's attitudes and actions, giving us, through ironic implication, the more "valid" interpretation of the events and their corresponding ideology. In the case of *Dom Casmurro*, one would think that the "implied author" would give us what Kermode calls the "skeptical" or "schismatic" perspective, which would attest to the validity of a more chaotic or arbitrary reality—mess over myth. But that is not exactly what happens with the novel. One of the main reasons it does not happen is that there is very little space in which an "implied author" can operate. Implying something requires not saying it explicitly. The ironic implied author functions best when the narrator is limited in understanding or intelligence. The pseudo-author must be capable of misinterpretation, or at least incomplete interpretation, so that the fuller reading can be implied. This critical, distanced, fuller reading is of course what irony is all about. The fascinating problem with *Dom Casmurro* is that its narrator is highly intelligent, critical, and self-conscious. Rather than leaving room for that other, implied author to provide an ironic critique of his attitudes, he does so himself. Hence there is a paradoxical situation much like the infamous "liar paradox" ("I am lying"), in which the person supposedly giving an invalid account is the same person calling the account invalid. As I will show, this paradox makes for a novel in which the notion of relativity is carried to its logical extreme, so that the validity of relativity itself becomes relative.

In a sense, this is a book of myth criticism. However, I wish to make it clear that it operates on a different level from many books of this sort. While I recognize that *Dom Casmurro* is ultimately Machado's creation, it is more to the point to show how the *narrator* displays a mythic mentality in this book. The narrator is very much a divided soul in whom the system-builder and the skeptic are at odds. Only by examining that mind-set in the narrator and recognizing its contradictions can we draw conclusions about the book's real meanings. I will be applying some of the methods of myth critics, a technique which implies at least a provisional acceptance of some assumptions that have lately come under attack. I hope that it will be realized that, just as the mythic aspects of the novel are separated from the true author, the so-called myth-criticism of this book, by being directed at one side of the mentality of a fictional character, is likewise detached from a more critical voice. In a sense this book presents the writings of a myth critic in a fairly traditional sense who looks for archetypes and who reads Bento Santiago as the nostalgic lover; additionally, it presents the work of a more "skeptical" critic who is more interested in how myth is displaced and who reads a more dubious Bento Santiago.

Dom Casmurro does not immediately strike one as being a mythic work. There is very little that explicitly invites mythic analysis, as in *Ulysses,* or that suggests the supernatural character of myth, as in *One Hundred Years of Solitude.* However, I am convinced that readers with a cooperative spirit will find with me many pleasingly subtle evidences of a distant correspondence with mythic discourse. The great distance between the underlying myth and the literary representation is an important and necessary matter, for it reinforces the sense of tension and alienation in modernity which is one of the main themes of the novel.

This book's title, borrowed from one of the narrator's own laments, which is discussed in chapter 2, is intended to suggest the displacement of myth in the modern world. The word "dreams" suggests the wishful, freely fantasizing quality of myth, while the word "retired" (*aposentados*) should be taken to signify both distancing and the modern bureaucratic classification for those who tend to be considered no longer useful. Its essays revolve around the work's tension between two opposing modes of thought: a primitive mentality, which favors the timeless, the absolute, and the ideal; and a modern mentality, which acknowledges a much more transitory and contingent reality.

This book consists of more or less self-contained studies, written over a period of several years. In a sense, it is a complement and continuation of a chapter dedicated to *Dom Casmurro* in my book, *Reversible Readings: Ambiguity in Four Modern Latin American Novels*. There I suggested that the novel is quite ambiguous but that it does not allow us to draw any conclusions about whether life is inherently ambiguous, or language necessarily equivocal. Here I will arrive at a similar ambivalence and claim that that in itself is a valid conclusion.

While I believe my approach will shed new light upon important areas of the novel and show how seemingly anomalous passages contribute to the work's coherence, I emphasize that this is simply one view among many and that if there is a last word on *Dom Casmurro*, it must be that there is no last word.

CHAPTER ONE

Myth and Its Transformations

Like many great novels, Machado de Assis' *Dom Casmurro*[1] resists classification. This is appropriate since the difficulty of categorizing is a principal theme of the work itself. The most important characters, Bentinho and Capitu, practically beg to be judged and yet are almost impossible to assess conveniently. Are Bentinho's suspicion, jealousy, and eventual bitterness justified, or is his own imagination his worst enemy? Is Capitu, his adolescent sweetheart and wife, a cunning social climber and heartless adulteress, or merely the innocent (if somewhat manipulative) victim of repression? The enigmas surrounding these two characters are the source of a cascade of other mysteries, involving every level of the novel, which ask to be solved but at the same time resist resolution in any categorical terms.

I believe that the most important conclusion to be drawn about the novel in recent years is that, when posed in conventional terms, certain questions are undecidable. The question of Capitu's guilt or innocence, for example, has been a perpetual stumbling block because many readers have thought it necessary to conclude one way or the other and have encountered evidence supporting both propositions. Over the past several years, however, we have gradually adjusted ourselves to the idea that the ambiguity of the question is one of the central points of the work. What is important is not to choose sides in the debate but to acknowledge the existence of the dichotomy. Gradually, we are beginning to see *Dom Casmurro* and Machado's other works as plays between great opposing forces in which the truth lies not at one pole or the other but somewhere in the middle.

Realism and Anti-Realism

We encounter similar problems of classification when we try to account for *Dom Casmurro* as a novel among other novels. If pressed to assign the work to a literary movement, most experts will associate it with nineteenth-century realism. After doing so, most will immediately begin qualifying that classification, for while the novel shows an interest in contemporary times, urban settings, middle-class characters, and bourgeois preoccupations, it only goes so far in conforming to the typical realistic mold. In many other respects, the novel seems not only to be outside the scope of realism but in fact to run directly counter to it. If *Dom Casmurro* fits into the set of qualities defining the movement, it fits like a stodgy old gentleman who knows that he deserves special treatment. The book shuns the ready-to-wear pattern and demands the tailor-made.

Massaud Moisés, probably as skillful a tailor as any, refers to a special division of the realistic movement to accommodate the Brazilian master and a few other figures. He places Machado within the stream of *interior* realism as opposed to the more common manifestation of *exterior* realism. Psychological penetration is the principal goal of interior realism. If it has finely detailed descriptions, they tend to be applied to memory rather than setting. Action and dialog give way to hesitation, reticence, and insinuations. In short, the narrative drama takes place in the psyche of the characters rather than in their parlors, opera houses, or train stations.[2]

We cannot help but accept the validity of Moisés' definition. But at the same time, we should regard the distinction between interior and exterior realism as one of tendencies rather than rigid categories. In spite of what Moisés would occasionally ask us to believe, there are many characteristics of *external* realism in *Dom Casmurro*. The critic speaks of the

"paupérrima presença da cidade . . . carioca" (extremely mea-
ger presence of the city of Rio)[3] in his works. In the case of *Dom
Casmurro*, this must be considered an exaggeration since we
find reference to Engenho Novo, Tijuca, Glória; to the Passeio
Público, the trains, the beach, the backyard walls, and many
other details of the city. The setting is unmistakably Rio de
Janeiro.[4] Moisés says that the Brazilian character of the works
is "apenas por acaso" (only by chance).[5] It would not seem to be
mere accident that in *Dom Casmurro* the protagonist is thrown
into the story's conflict because of a bit of folk catholicism—a
promise to God—or that the conflict is substantially (if not
finally) settled by a rather ingenious "jeitinho"—the sponsor-
ship of a substitute in the priesthood. These motifs, essential to
the novel, are also essentially Brazilian.

Machado's fidelity to his urban setting and to Brazilian reality are not the only factors that could identify *Dom Casmurro*
as a realistic novel in the normally accepted sense. The novel
is abundantly populated with typical representatives of the
bourgeoisie: interim administrators, lawyers, businessmen,
and section heads. It also follows the realistic norm of concern
with the contemporary scene. References to modes of transportation, important figures such as the emperor, and current
events such as the Crimean War identify the novel, from the
point of view of the contemporary reading public, as "modern."

In a sense, *Dom Casmurro* is distinguishable from other realistic novels more by a difference of degree than by a difference
of kind. It contains the same "realistic" detail, but the detail is
not *accumulated* as much as in many realistic novels. Machado
acknowledges the esthetic of the "livro omisso" (book with
omissions—chap. 59). On the other hand, we would not be completely fair if we did not admit, along with Massaud Moisés, a
difference in kind. Surely Machado is more interested in the
internal conflicts of his characters than in their external vicissitudes. He is more properly an analyst of the individual than
of society. Furthermore, most would agree that Machado is able
to instill in his protagonists a universality that transcends the
"here-and-now" orientation traditionally assigned to the real-
ists. To quote Moisés, the characters "são . . . mais símbolos de
dramas coletivos ou universais do que expressões típicas de
certo 'meio' cultural e temporal" (are . . . more symbols of collective or universal dramas than typical expressions of a certain
cultural and temporal 'milieu').[6]

Perhaps one of the most important differences of kind in *Dom Casmurro* is a particular attitude about contemporary reality. That reality, it would seem, exists in the novel not as an object that attracts and fascinates the narrator but rather as a kind of counterpoint serving to define a more desirable existence completely separated from modernity. One of the constants of the novel is the narrator's preference for the old over the new: "Uso louça velha e mobília velha" (I use old china and old furniture—chap. 2); "Os sonhos antigos foram aposentados . . . a ilha dos sonhos, como a dos amores, como todas as ilhas de todos os mares, são agora objeto da ambição e da rivalidade da Europa e dos Estados Unidos" (The old dreams have been retired. . . . the isle of dreams, like the isle of love, and all the isles of all the seas, are now the object of the ambition and rivalry of Europe and the United States—chap. 64); ". . . um lenço bastou a acender os ciúmes de Otelo e compor a mais sublime tragédia deste mundo. Os lenços perderam-se, hoje são precisos os próprios lençóis" (. . . a handkerchief was enough to kindle the jealousy of Othello and fashion the most sublime tragedy of this world. Handkerchiefs have passed out of use; today one must have nothing less than sheets—chap. 135). According to a well-known definition by Baudelaire, "La modernité, c'est le transitoire, le fugitif, le contingent, la moité de l'art, dont l'autre moité est l'éternel et l'immuable" (Modernity is the transitory, the fugitive, the contingent—one half of art, of which the other half is the eternal and the immutable).[7] Machado, like Baudelaire, seems to conceive of modernity as half of a dichotomy, for he has the protagonist Bento Santiago sense profoundly that modernity represents a shocking compounding of changes and react strongly against it. Hence, *Dom Casmurro*'s narrator does not simply portray the modern world, he portrays a nostalgic critique of that world. Realism normally involves an embrace of modernity—a fascination (or at least coming-to-terms) with the rapidity, commotion, and changeable conditions that constitute the modern world. The narrator's voice is decidedly anti-modernist. Since the validity of that voice is ambiguous (Bento may or may not be deluded), we conclude that the implied author (as opposed to the narrator) is ambivalent when it comes to realism. He is realist and anti-realist at the same time. Machado's conflicts have a lot to do with characters who are inevitably placed in the contemporary world but at the same time out of place in that setting.

The Applicability and Limitations of Myth Criticism

One of the critical approaches best suited for comprehending this dialectic in literature between the old and the new, the primitive and the modern (and one relatively new to Machadian criticism[8]), is myth criticism. It may be a bit deceptive to refer to "myth criticism" singularly when in fact there are several different directions that might be designated by such a term. The particular direction of this study consists of examining the relationship between literature, as a highly stylized, differentiated, and cultured expression, and myth as a more prototypical, primitive, and undifferentiated form.

As a working definition of myth, we may adopt the following by Bernice Slote: "Myth . . . is the narrative form of those particularly archetypal symbols which together make a coherent revelation of what man knows and what he believes."[9] This definition has three important things to say about myth: (1) it is a story, (2) the motifs that compose it are archetypes, and (3) it involves truths or beliefs. We may define archetypes as universal motifs, or motifs that tend to be found in the narrative expressions of many cultures. Types or themes such as the great mother as the source of all life, the wise old man who gives vital orientation to the younger initiate, the descent into the underworld, and the regeneration of life are examples of archetypes. We may call them archetypes because literature is replete with versions of such motifs. As we can see from these few examples, these so-called archetypes relate to some of our most profound beliefs concerning life, death, good, and evil. They frequently involve the supernatural; therefore, we talk about how they reveal beliefs or unquestioned truths and find a close association between archetypes and religion. They also relate to some of the most basic and universal experiences of life.

I do not want to use the term "universal" in an absolute sense, for while there are certain themes or patterns that approach ubiquity, I would hesitate to claim that they belong to every culture. Surely I could not prove such a claim. In employing the word "universal," I wish to preserve some of its etymological suggestion of *turning toward oneness*.

I will treat *Dom Casmurro* as an outgrowth and a transformation of myth. Ingenuous, folkloric narratives may abound with fantastic or supernatural elements and contain superhuman characters. These primitive stories have few transformations and would be considered relatively close to the conception of myth. More artistic or learned stories contain more realistic characters and avoid the supernatural in favor of what is plausible in a modern, scientific sense. These stories are relatively far removed from myth and would seem to be the product of more transformations. The concept of myth, based on archetypes, and the concept of literary expression as a transformation (or "displacement" in the terminology of Northrop Frye[10]) of myth, are thus ways of taking into account the universals and particulars of literature. In the case of *Dom Casmurro,* these concepts should help us identify the concerns it shares with great world literature and also help define how those universals reveal themselves in an individual style. I will concentrate particularly upon the processes that transform the myth into a modern novel. In addition, the approach should help us account for some of the novel's important conceptual dichotomies—the essential vs. the relative, the primitive vs. the modern, and the nonrealistic vs. the realistic—to the extent that we can identify the former element in each dichotomy with the primal, mythic component, and the latter element with the displaced contemporary reality.

Having mentioned some ways in which I feel myth criticism is applicable to literary study in general and Machado's novel in particular, I would like to say a few words about some of the potential misuses of myth criticism and how I propose to avoid them.

The approach can often be criticized for making idealistic claims for itself as a method for comprehending literature. Most of these criticisms have to do with unproved (and unprovable) claims about the universality of myths and archetypes and their status as matrices of literature as a whole.[11] I share some of these doubts about the absolute universality of myths and feel that it would be a mistake to apply a single formula of analysis (mythic or not) to any and all works. At the same time, it seems apparent that certain mythical patterns are extremely common. When these structures are present in a given work, especially when they are disguised, identification of such patterns can often be enlightening. Since I am examining a single novel in the light of a single myth, I will have no reason to become involved in the question of the general efficacy of myth criticism, or the ubiquity of myth *per se.*

Often myth criticism deteriorates into mystification—unverifiable speculation about contents of a collective unconscious or deep, emotional chords struck with readers or authors.[12] I view this sort of psychologizing as a distraction from the proper aim of criticism, which is to examine the experience of literature by means of textual evidence, and will try to avoid the temptation to be an amateur psychologist.

The evocation of myth has unfortunately been linked at times with questionable ideological biases. For example, the conquering that often occurs in myth, when called an eternal or essential pattern of behavior, might tend to validate an attitude of domination and repression. Making an institution of the mythic return to origins can be used to support reactionary thinking.[13] We will see that Bentinho uses myth in some of these very ways. I will call attention to these misuses as they occur and show how they are questioned by the novel itself, but I hope to avoid them in my own practice.

Finally, myth criticism can sometimes be criticized for being static, that is, for identifying themes and motifs but failing to show how such identification helps our understanding of works or how the elements function.[14] This shortcoming is often the result of devoting excessive attention to the myths and archetypes themselves and not enough attention to the processes that account for the literary derivation of a particular work from its mythic basis. To show how I intend to avoid this pitfall, I will attempt to outline my method of analysis in more detail.

A "Grammar" of Literature

The efficacy of any critical approach may be judged by its ability to explain literature as a system. We might define a system as any type of organization that functions according to rules. Therefore, critical approaches have validity insofar as they are able to identify and demonstrate the rules by which works operate. Myth criticism properly conceptualized seems to possess this capability. To resort to a common analogy, a critical approach should be a kind of "grammar" of literature, demonstrating the constitutional rules of texts the way linguists explain the rules by which language operates.[15] My approach, like that of many others, is very roughly analogous to a kind of generative grammar:[16] I will postulate that the actual representation of the text derives from a more abstract, underlying structure. The primitive narrative forms we call myths often provide the rough outline for literary texts, being devoid of detail or individual style in much the same way that a crude sketch may suggest the general contours of a building. The actual design of the literary work, which could be compared to a detailed blueprint of the building, involves supplying specific information and transforming the underlying myth to a greater or lesser degree. The process of modification is accomplished, as in the linguistic model, by applying certain transformational rules. For my purposes in this book, I will propose the existence of four transforming devices—metaphor, metonymy, synecdoche, and irony, or the so-called four major tropes.

According to this model, derivation of a work of literature from myth is a process of supplying specific data (regarding setting, characters, and so forth) and using these basic literary devices. A great deal of creativity and individual variation are possible within this mechanism; the tropes can be bypassed entirely or used repeatedly. Lesser application of the tropes yields fantastic narratives; greater application yields realistic ones.

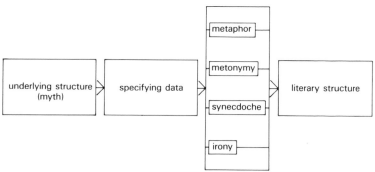

Fig 1.1: Generating literature from myth

We will see that *Dom Casmurro* is characterized by extensive use of the transforming devices and that consequently there is a considerable distance between the surface, textual representation and the underlying myth. I will later treat the major tropes in some detail, but first I wish to establish the novel's connection with a particular type of narrative.

The Model of Heroic Narrative

Bento Santiago is no hero in any traditional sense. However, it is important to realize that *as a narrator* he has a great deal to do with heroism.

Dom Casmurro is fiction in the guise of autobiography. In composing his memoirs, Santiago is not a passive transcriber of a prefabricated history but rather an active inventor of his own self. One recent study of autobiography describes the situation appropriately:

> The autobiographer may summon memory to his aid, amended and corrected by data such as letters and diaries, and begin to write about himself, but his muse, Mnemosyne, is an artist, his data are inadequate, his perception is partial. His role is essentially that of interpreter and coordinator, and his "actual events" become "virtual events" in the process of writing. Fiction, in other words, ensnares reality from the beginning.[17]

Inescapably, autobiographers are narrators, and they are bound by the practices of story telling. This form of writing may be historical, but it is also rhetorical, and its tools of narration are the same as those of fiction. In fact, as one critic of autobiography states, ". . . the self that is at the center of all autobiographical narrative is necessarily a fictive structure."[18] As a book of fiction masked as autobiography, *Dom Casmurro* is a fiction of a fiction. In fact, it could be read quite fruitfully as a book about writing memoirs.

The narrator must be influenced by conventional procedures. One of the most powerful conventions, which has a profound effect upon the shaping of the account, is that of genre. Santiago could conceivably tell his story as a tragedy, a comedy, a farce, an epic, or as any other of the traditional forms. An early chapter of the novel (9), wherein an old tenor tells Santiago that life is an opera and Santiago replies that it might just as well be a sea voyage or a battle, can easily be read as a metafictional statement about how humans must resort to some sort of narrative genre to comprehend life. (The narrator might have proposed that life was an epic, for sea voyages and battles are the traditional stock of that type of narrative.) So what genre does Santiago choose for his autobiography?

He appears to accept the tenor's assertion that life is an opera (chap. 10), and to some extent Bentinho's written "life" could be read as such. This is especially true if we think of the word "opera" in its more general, etymologic sense as simply a "work." But what kind of "opera" would this life be? Generic distinctions are often made on the basis of the personality of the protagonist, and Santiago's work is no exception. At various points, the narrator compares himself with characters in assorted narratives. In chapter 135 he is Othello; in chapter

34 he is Columbus, discovering America. In chapter 33 Capitu is Thetis, which could easily make the narrator Adamastor by implication (more on this in chapter 5). When he is about to commit suicide (chap. 136), he tries to give himself courage by comparing himself to Cato, who in turn had compared himself to Plato. Some of these figures belong to epics, some to historiography, some to tragic drama or opera, or both. But they all have certain qualities in common—greatness, power, seriousness, charisma—in short, they are all somehow heroic. Santiago chooses a narrative form for his autobiography which adheres to the tradition of heroic discourse.

Since little of his life bears any direct resemblance to that model, Santiago must resort to certain rhetorical procedures in his narration, establishing and reestablishing the connection between the facts of his life and the model for his narration. Chapter 55, concerning Bentinho's failed attempt at writing a sonnet, is a good example. Only two lines are ever written: "Oh! flor do céu! oh! flor cândida e pura!" (O flower of heaven! O flower bright and pure), and "Perde-se a vida, ganha-se a batalha!" (Life is lost, the battle is still won!). The boy never writes the lines connecting the beginning and the end, but the narrator establishes a clear connection for the reader between Capitu, the obvious referent of the first line, and a tragic but transcendent battle. Not only in this case, but over and over again, the facts of the relationship with Capitu are imaginatively connected to a tradition of heroic discourse.

This is not an isolated phenomenon in *Dom Casmurro*, as Enylton de Sá Rego has pointed out quite persuasively.[19] It is also especially pervasive in the two other novels which, along with *Dom Casmurro*, are normally considered to be Machado's greatest. Helen Caldwell finds echoes of *Oedipus* and *Macbeth* in *Memórias póstumas de Brás Cubas* and in particular emphasizes how the narrator explicitly compares his life with the warlike exploits of Virgil's Aeneas.[20] In *Quincas Borba*, the comparison between the protagonist and the master of war, Napoleon, could hardly be more obvious, for at the end of the book the central character actually crowns himself in direct imitation of the French emperor.

In all three novels there is a persistent "heroization" of the narrative through figurative language (I will demonstrate this in *Dom Casmurro* presently). Allusions to other literary works abound, and more often than not the intertextual context woven by these references involves grandiose or heroic works.

But the conformity to heroic models is not a simple one, for it both asserts and negates itself. Chapter 73, which expounds the idea that destiny is both a dramatist and a stage manager, demonstrates the complexity of the correspondence. The narrator compares certain events in his life with a play he once attended:

> . . . representou-se . . . um drama que acabava pelo juízo final. O principal personagem era Asaverus, que no último quadro concluía um monólogo por esta exclamação: "Ouço a trombeta do arcanjo!" Não se ouviu trombeta nenhuma. Asaverus, envergonhado, repetiu a palavra, agora mais alto, para advertir o contra-regra, mas ainda nada. Então caminhou para o fundo, disfarçadamente trágico, mas efetivamente com o fim de falar ao bastidor, e dizer em voz surda: "O pistão! o pistão! o pistão!" O público ouviu esta palavra e desatou a rir, até que, quando a trombeta soou deveras, a Asaverus bradou pela terceira vez que era a do arcanjo, um gaiato da platéia corrigiu cá de baixo: "Não, senhor, é o pistão do arcanjo!"

> . . . they performed here . . . a drama that ended with the Last Judgment. The principal character was Ahasuerus, who, in the last scene, concluded a monologue with this exclamation, "I hear the trumpet of the archangel!" No trumpet was heard at all. Ahasuerus, covered with shame, repeated the line, this time louder, to cue the stage manager, but still nothing. Then he walked toward the back, under a pretense of tragic gesture, but actually for the purpose of whispering into the wings, "The cornet! the cornet! the cornet!" The audience caught this word and burst into laughter, so that when the trumpet sounded in earnest and Ahasuerus shouted for the third time that it was that of the archangel, a little urchin in the pit corrected him from here below, "No, senhor, it is the archangel's cornet!" (chap. 73)

The protagonist in this presentation is assigned a tragic, heroic role. However, the circumstances of the realization of that role make it seem ludicrously unconvincing. Similarly, Bento Santiago casts his narrative in the heroic mold and assigns himself the main part. But incongruous circumstances work against his successfully playing that role.

Dom Casmurro presents a constant going and coming between an underlying "script," which could be called the heroic quest, and an incongruous "performance" of that script, which is the protagonist's actual life. This book will focus not only on the elements of the script and the performance but also on the mechanisms that permit our perception to move back and forth between the two.

The Quest Myth

While there may be several myths, probably the most important to literary study, and the only one to concern us here, is the myth of the hero's adventure, or the quest myth. There is some feeling that this myth is central to all myths or that all other myths are appendages to the quest. Joseph Campbell refers to the heroic adventure as the "monomyth," and Northrop Frye calls the quest *the* central, controlling mythic structure of literature. Vladimir Propp claims that the quest constitutes an underlying structure for practically all Russian folktales, and in applying his tools of analysis to widely differing texts, others have implied that the theory holds for all narrative.[21] That may or may not be so. All I intend to show here is that the quest myth is an underlying basis for *Dom Casmurro*. Campbell says that the quest myth has three essential stages: separation, initiation, and return. He elaborates: "A hero ventures forth from the world of common day into a region of supernatural wonder: fabulous forces are there encountered and a decisive victory is won: the hero comes back from this mysterious adventure with the power to bestow boons on his fellow men."[22] Already we begin to see that the concept of the quest myth, as it is treated in practice, does not have a single level of specificity. The mythic structure may have various degrees of detail or elaboration, but the entire content should somehow be subsumed in the tripartite structure of separation, initiation, and return.

Campbells' study discusses several other archetypal motifs commonly found within the controlling structure of the quest myth. There is often a call to adventure which induces the hero, voluntarily or otherwise, to begin his quest. A helper, often in the form of a wise old man or woman, gives the hero needed orientation as he embarks. His separation from society is generally marked by the crossing of some significant threshold. Once the separation is accomplished, the hero commonly faces severe tests which threaten his life, and at times he seems even to die. Even so, he eventually triumphs over his enemy, often with magical aid from another helper. He is occasionally rewarded with a sacred marriage to a supernatural goddess. Often he secures a magic elixir that will cure and benefit society. His departure from the region of trials frequently involves a flight from sinister forces. He commonly crosses another threshold as he returns to society. As he returns, he often has a renewed quality, as if he had been resurrected, and frequently he transfers this revitalization to his community.[23]

If we turn our minds back to *Dom Casmurro*, we should begin to sense a vague correspondence between the novel's narrative structure and the quest myth. We notice that Bentinho's realization that he is in love with Capitu amounts to a kind of call to adventure—to the adventure of love, or perhaps life itself. This realization also causes a separation from society, which in Bentinho's case is primarily his family. Curiously, the moment of separation is literally associated with a threshold—that of the parlor, or "sala de visitas," which Bentinho almost enters before he hears the family talking about him and hides behind a door (chap. 3). Bentinho faces a series of trials—the impediments to marrying Capitu because of his mother's promise to God to make him a priest, plus several tribulations in his relationship with Capitu. He enters the seminary against his will and endures there a period of death-like acquiescence and stultification. He encounters a helper in his friend Escobar, who is a sort of "wizard" with numbers and other calculations and whose advice is responsible for Bentinho's triumph over the seminary and over his mother's debt to God. Bentinho returns to the society of his family, and his triumph culminates in a wedding to the "goddess" Capitu.

Literary Transformations in *Dom Casmurro*

After this brief outline of mythic elements in *Dom Casmurro*, two things should be apparent. First, there is considerable distance or displacement between the original concept of the quest myth and the actual narrative realization of the novel. Second, the correspondence with the three phases of the hero's quest only covers the first part of the novel, up to the moment of the wedding. Actually, the second part also corresponds, but as I will explain shortly, it corresponds in a negative rather than a positive way. I will attempt to show what these important phenomena have to do with our "literary grammar" of myth criticism. As I mentioned, the narrative as expressed derives from the underlying structure of myth by means of the application of transformational rules. It might be possible to follow the example of linguists and a few literary critics and define a detailed list of transformational procedures. To do so, however, would provide me with a theory far more powerful than I really want. For my purposes, I find that criticism is already endowed with an adequate set of "rules"—the traditionally accepted rhetorical devices. It is my hypothesis that the four *major tropes*—metaphor, metonymy, synecdoche, and irony[24]—will account for practically all the transformations that take place between myth and Machado's modern novel.

I will now try to show how each of the four major tropes may operate in the displacement of myth. I do this more by way of demonstration at this point than in the name of providing a coherent or systematic explication of the novel as a whole.

Metaphor

In the trial phase of an undisplaced quest myth, the hero often travels through a threatening natural setting, such as the sea. *Dom Casmurro* preserves the sea quest, in a highly transformed manner, through metaphor. Besides comparing himself to Columbus (chap. 34), the narrator equates his life with a sea voyage (chap. 9). He recounts a moment of profound crisis in his relationship with Capitu "como um marujo contaria o seu naufrágio" (as an old sailor recalls his shipwreck—chap. 132) and refers to loving as navigating a stormy sea (chap. 49). By means of such metaphors, Bentinho is able to lead a realistic, citified existence and at the same time preserve vestiges of the ocean adventurer.

The unfinished sonnet already mentioned involves a metaphor. The act of fighting with words, as well as the meaning of the words themselves, are a subtle figure based upon the sword/pen comparison. Here again, this metaphor preserves a heroic dimension but transforms it so that it fits into an unthreatening and unheroic situation.

The hero embarking upon his adventure often receives valuable counsel from a wise old man or woman. Just after Bentinho stumbles out of his house with the realization that he loves Capitu, he receives imagined counsel from a personified coconut tree. Here an archetype of the hero's adventure is metaphorically displaced so that its suggestion colors the novel but its real existence is only in the imagination of a star-struck lad.

Metonymy

The idea of displacement is implied in the definition of metonymy, so the device is particularly appropriate for the displacement from myth to realism. In *Dom Casmurro*, metonymy permits Bentinho to be exempt from certain trials of the mythic hero, at the same time preserving the suggestion of these trials. In myth, the hero usually experiences a physical bout with the forces of death. In *Dom Casmurro*, Bentinho contends with death as well, but this battle is transferred to something associated or contiguous. For example, Bentinho's stay in the seminary represents the culmination of his "testing period," but there is very little physically threatening about the experience. During his weekends, however, he experiences a displaced bout with death in his encounter with the young leper, Manduca. Manduca's experience with death is of course much more concrete than Bentinho's at that moment. The coincidence of the encounter between the two young men and Bentinho's stay in the seminary allows some of Manduca's morbid struggle to "rub off" onto Bentinho.

Another important instance in which metonymy creates realistic displacement is the development of the idea that one's own life is preserved through one's offspring. Having progeny is of the utmost importance to Bentinho. When Capitu chides him with the idea that he will become a priest and she will bear another man's child, Bentinho is stupified and sees his lack of progeny as his own "aniquilação" (annihilation–chap. 45). Bentinho thus experiences a distant version of the hero's supreme trial, without ever encountering physical danger.

Synecdoche

In myth the hero may travel through a threatening oceanic world. He is apt to have an encounter with a beautiful woman within this mythic world. By exchanging the part for the whole, *Dom Casmurro* preserves this mythic element within a modern setting. Capitu is not a part of the dreadful sea world; instead, she carries that fearful world as part of her through the important image of her "olhos de ressaca" (undertow eyes—chap. 32). Once again, this device permits Bentinho to undergo a series of dangerous tests in a figurative rather than a literal sense.

But this is not the only function of the synecdoche. The experience of the hero tends to be one of totality. He may travel the whole world, see in a vision the entire course of history, or somehow experience all that has ever been felt. The transfer in

Dom Casmurro from woman-within-the-world to world-within-the-woman allows for an encyclopedic dimension in the novel. Capitu may thus be seen as a microcosm. Bentinho's troubled relationship with her may assume the mythic suggestion of an encounter with the totality of life itself, with the world, or with the cosmos.

Irony

Irony is an implied negation. A type of irony which is especially applicable as a literary transformation of myth is what we might call role irony. In this context it consists of assigning a particular character a mythic or heroic role on the one hand and assigning to him on the other hand attributes that are the negation of that role.

For example, the "agregado" or live-in dependent, José Dias, having agreed to assist in extracting Bentinho from the obligation to become a priest, would correspond to the archetypal role of the wise old helper. However, in his actual characterization he is so inept and impractical that he is anything but helpful. The surface attributes of ineptitude and amiable foolishness and the underlying mythic role of wise helper are in ironic juxtaposition, and José Dias emerges as a sort of anti-helper.

The same type of irony clearly operates in the case of Bentinho. According to the underlying mythic dimension of the novel, Bentinho is assigned to the role of hero. But in reality he is petty, insecure, and weak. True mythic heroes do not stutter, shrink from riding horseback, or fail miserably in writing sonnets. Furthermore, he is bound to modernity. Real mythic heroes do not live in the suburbs, buy coconut candy from street vendors, or fall asleep on trains. Subtly, archetypal motifs associate Bentinho with the hero on his quest for the absolute. At the same time, the realistic details of his character and situation tell us he is small and quite unheroic. We ironically perceive him as an anti-hero because of the coincidence of these opposing messages. This irony seems to be a major factor in creating a considerable distance in the novel between myth and the modern reality of the characters.

A Structural Irony

The sense of transformation, distance, and irony created by the role negation just examined is strengthened by a structural irony, encompassing the last part of the novel. As I brought out earlier, the quest myth, with its three essential phases of separation, initiation, and return, corresponds with the first part of the novel, culminating in Bentinho and Capitu's marriage. The remainder of the novel takes this structure, which starts and ends with the hero's integration with the community, and duplicates it ironically so that there are actually two mythic cycles—an affirmative one followed by a negative one.

It is some time after his wedding that Bentinho experiences his second, ironic call to adventure. This time it is a call to suspicion, jealousy, and resentment instead of to love and hope. The beginning of this adventure, as with the first one, is signalled by the crossing of a threshold. Bentinho goes to the opera one night, leaving Capitu at home, and upon returning discovers Escobar "à porta do corredor" (at the front door—chap 113). He crosses the threshold into a transformed, bitter world. Bentinho's voyage of discovery takes him deeper and deeper into the underworld, imaginary or real, of monstrosities, treachery, and nothingness. As before, Escobar assumes the role of the helper. This time, however, the role is played with irony, for Escobar urges him into a bottomless pit. Even after his death, Escobar's spectre spurs Bentinho to go deeper and deeper. This second, ironic adventure brings about Bentinho's separation from his wife and more generally from his entire society and even himself.

He becomes Dom Casmurro, "homem calado e metido consigo" (a morose, tight-lipped man withdrawn within himself—chap. 1). The best he can do in his condition is to accomplish a sour negation of modernity, which he associates with his current stagnation, and to write a nostalgic memoir evoking better times through subtly mythic discourse. The book constitutes the final return phase of the protagonist/narrator's mythic cycle. Again, though, it is an ironic return—not the triumphant homecoming of a hero, but a regress that trumpets its own failure, proclaiming the impossibility of true return and the failure of its own efforts to achieve such a goal.

CHAPTER TWO

The Abolition of Time

For several years, critics have been studying the function of time in the works of Machado de Assis—time as a central thematic motif, as an element in the psychological delineation of characters, and as a structuring principle for narration.[1] One perspective of time that has not received adequate attention from Machadian scholars is the mythic perspective.

In the last chapter I tried to demonstrate that, albeit in a considerably disguised manner, *Dom Casmurro* participates in the ancient tradition of fantastic and heroic stories that we call myths. Particularly, I identified its affinity with the quest myth, which generally includes a decisive battle between the hero and some phantasmagoric being. This chapter will analyze the function of time as the antagonist in that duel.

Time as a "Dragon"

For a point of departure in this analysis, I will refer to the final words of Dirce Cortes Riedel's important book, *O tempo no romance machadiano:* "Personagem ativa ou clima asfixiante, gerador de inquietações e dúvidas, o tempo paradoxal, dragão que o homem mata ou nutre, é eixo do romance machadiano. . . . " (Active character or asphyxiating climate, breeder of inquietude and doubts—the paradox of time, dragon that man kills or nurtures, is the axis of the Machadian novel. . . .)[2]

Some fascinating concepts are suggested here although they are not developed in the book. The first of these is that time can be personified and assume the role of a character in a literary work. The second is an extension of the first: that time can be, rather than personified, made an animal or even transformed into a monster. Time can be, within a literary work, a "dragon." Since the dragon is a fantastic and mythic being, it is implied that the behavior of other characters in the face of time may acquire the dimensions of the hero's battle against some evil, supernatural monster.

At first glance *Dom Casmurro* may seem to be the most distant work imaginable from that marvelous kingdom of beings which are, if not deified, then surely superhuman. What do interim administrations, spats, and homeopathic medicine have to do with myth? On the surface, *Dom Casmurro* is a supremely bourgeois work. The narrator, Bento Santiago, says that before writing his own memoirs, he considered composing a *História dos Subúrbios,* and in the final analysis the history he eventually wrote is not so far from it. It concerns an urban setting and domestic preoccupations: boulevards, weddings, tea with priests, pounds sterling, and so forth. One of the plot's central concerns is adultery. The domestic nature of this theme, be the adultery an actual offense realized by Capitu or simply a mental exaggeration on the part of Bentinho, identifies the novel with the tradition of the bourgeois novel,[3] of which *Madame Bovary* is a well-known example. Let us remember also Santiago's stated motive for writing his book: "Ora, como tudo cansa, esta monotonia acabou por exaurir-me também. Quis variar, e lembrou-me escrever um livro" (But, as everything wearies one, this monotony too finally exhausted me. I wanted a change. What if I wrote a book?—chap. 2). A book written to escape tedium would seem to be a petty and common work, and one would think that it would display very little similarity with a mythic quest. But we must recognize that this urban and suburban world, with its local color and modern concerns, is just one part of the novel's context. The homey trifles are merely the most visible, accessible extremity of the work. Beneath this superficial tip, there is an iceberg that descends into the depths of myth.

And who will be our mythic hero, if not Bentinho Santiago, that eater of coconut candy and writer of unfinished sonnets? Petty as he may seem, Bentinho possesses an underlying dimension that identifies him with a long tradition of heroic figures. In his attitude toward time, Bentinho demonstrates an anachronistic predisposition. Rather than exhibiting a modern mentality, he often shows what Mircea Eliade and others call a "primitive mentality."[4] Fleeing the inexorable succession of chronological time in which each moment is unique and unrepeatable, primitive men sought to attain a state outside worldly time. By various means they tried to abolish "profane time" and to create the impression of "mythic time," profound, stable, and infinite. Achieving the state of mythic time, these men, according to Eliade, had the sensation of having returned to the beginning of time and of man, of having annihilated all succession and individual distinction among beings. They participated in a singular and primordial pattern and in so doing felt immortal. As we will see, Bentinho seems to share this primitive mentality; he exhibits the propensity to try to overcome profane time and to attain sacred or mythic time. Occasionally, he assumes the posture of that mythic hero, locked in a supreme battle with the monster. In his case, the ogre is time itself, and his duel is, so to speak, a fight to the death.

Of course there is a metaphor involved here which defines time in a particular way. Metaphor is one of the chief means by which we comprehend abstractions.[5] There are several common metaphors used to define our concept of time—for example, time as a river or some other flowing substance, time as a traveler, time as a space through which to travel, time as money, time as a machine, and time as an adversary or predator. Expressions such as "Time caught up with her," and "He's losing the race with time" are based upon the time-as-predator metaphor. Perhaps more than any other means of conceptualizing time, the time-as-predator metaphor emphasizes that temporality derives from the physical reality of death.

Machado never has his narrator Dom Casmurro say in so many words that time is a devouring monster. However, he developed the metaphor quite explicitly in *Memórias póstumas de Brás Cubas*. In the masterful "O delírio" (The delirium), Brás Cubas has a frightening encounter with Nature, personified as Pandora. He asks her for a few more years of life, and receives the reply, "Pobre minuto! . . . Para que queres tu mais alguns instantes de vida? Para devorar e seres devorado depois?" (Pitiful minute! . . . Why do you want a few more instants of life? To devour and be later devoured?). He envisions the centuries smashing him between their fingernails and is told that "O minuto que vem é forte, jocundo, supõe trazer em si a eternidade, e traz a morte" (The coming moment is strong and jovial. It presumes to carry eternity within itself, and carries death).[6] In this earlier work, time is clearly defined as a living being, and one with monstrous qualities. I will try to show in this chapter that the time-as-predator metaphor is equally essential to the conceptual framework of *Dom Casmurro*. As a general rule, global abstractions in the novel such as life and destiny are either made animate or described as the work of some animate being. Life, for example, is an opera, with a libretto by God and a score by Satan (chap. 9). Destiny is a wily playwright (chap. 72) and an undependable stage manager (chap. 73). The narrator sums up his entire story with a personification of destiny as a cruel manipulator (using the verb "quis" to attribute will): ". . . a minha primeira amiga e o meu maior amigo . . . quis o destino que acabassem juntando-se e enganando-me" (. . . my first love and my greatest friend . . . destiny willed that they should join together and deceive me—chap. 148). The time-as-predator metaphor easily fits this general rule.

Besides being instrumental in the thematic richness of the work, the metaphor equating time and a monster allows for a transformation or displacement of the quest myth. Bentinho may lead an unheroic existence in a modern, realistic setting and at the same time participate figuratively in the tradition of dangerous, mythic adventure.

Weapons of a Primitive Mentality

Bentinho makes war against time on several occasions and in several ways. Normally he fails to emerge victorious, but once in a while he does seem to have some success. Let us now examine two moments in which he manages to surpass that irreversible time of the chronometers and to arrive at a state, however transient, of fixed and sacred time.

The first of these is when Bentinho combs Capitu's hair and they exchange their first kiss. Capitu's hair is a sort of anchor upon which Bentinho fixes all the importance of the moment.

He desires to preserve the instant of so many new sensations, prolonging that grooming session for an eternity. His aspiration, therefore, is that Capitu's tresses be unending:

> Os dedos roçavam na nuca da pequena ou nas espáduas vestidas de chita, e a sensação era um deleite. Mas, enfim, os cabelos iam acabando, por mais que eu os quisesse intermináveis. Não pedi ao céu que eles fossem tão longos como os de Aurora, porque não conhecia ainda esta divindade que os velhos poetas me apresentaram depois; mas, desejei penteá-los por todos os séculos dos séculos, tecer duas tranças que pudessem envolver o infinito por um número inominável de vezes.

> My fingers brushed along her neck or over the calico-covered shoulders, and the sensation was sweet. But finally her hair came to an end, however much I wished it interminable. I did not ask heaven that it might be as long as Aurora's, because I did not yet know this divinity which the old poets presented to me later; but I longed to comb it through all the ages of ages, to weave two braids that might enfold the infinite an unnameable number of times. (chap. 33)

A little before the combing, the young lovers' eyes meet. Bentinho experiences that moment, so memorable in the novel, of ecstasy and danger in Capitu's "olhos de ressaca" (undertow eyes). For the protagonist, this is a moment outside mundane time and one of the very few cases in which he conquers his "dragon": "Quantos minutos gastamos naquele jogo? Só os relógios do céu terão marcado esse tempo infinito e breve" (How many minutes did we pass in that game? Only the clocks of heaven will have noted this space of time which was infinite yet brief—chap. 32). The occasion of the first kiss also belongs to atemporal, sacred, and celestial time. To demonstrate how this instant is exempt from worldliness, the author refrains from representing it explicitly, giving instead an ellipsis that makes a jump from preparation to the consequence: ". . . ela abrochou os lábios, eu desci os meus, e ... Grande foi a sensação do beijo" (. . . she made a movement with her lips, I lowered mine, and ... The sensation of the kiss was immense—chap. 33).*

The newlyweds' honeymoon is another period when the protagonist succeeds in annihilating successive time. That paradisiacal moment is described in terms of an uncommon clock: "Imagina um relógio que só tivesse pêndulo, sem

---

*Unspaced suspension points are original in Machado's text.

mostrador, de maneira que não se vissem as horas escritas. O pêndulo iria de um lado para outro, mas nenhum sinal externo mostraria a marcha do tempo. Tal foi aquela semana da Tijuca" (Imagine a clock that had only a pendulum and no face, so that you did not see the hours marked. The pendulum would go from side to side, but no outward sign would show the march of time. This was the week on Tijuca—chap. 102).

Loving

Both in the case of the first kiss and in that of the honeymoon, the force responsible for the transcendence of profane time into mythic time is love. By means of love, Bentinho in rare moments achieves a victory over the devouring monster. Communion with another being is one primordial way of annulling individual existence and the mortality that it implies and of participating in a prototypical and eternal pattern. Bentinho was relishing such moments with Capitu, even when, as mere youngsters, they played priest and sacristan: "Estávamos ali com o céu em nós. As mãos, unindo os nervos, faziam das duas criaturas uma só, mas uma criatura seráfica" (We stood there with heaven in us. Our hands united our nerves, and made of two creatures one—and that one a seraph—chap. 14). Having experienced such heavenly flights, he naturally desires to repeat the sensation. This is the source of Capitu's enormous enchantment. Bentinho's backyard friend thus takes on far greater proportions than those of a girlfriend or wife. She represents the possibility, through love, of liberation from the world, from time, and from mortality. At times the narrator gives us a glimpse of the totalizing aspect of the loving enterprise. He points out, for example, that in doing a thousand Paternosters and a thousand Hail Marys, requesting exemption from the seminary and consequently the opportunity to marry Capitu, he was in reality asking for something much more inclusive: "Realmente, a matéria do benefício era agora imensa, não menos que a salvação ou o naufrágio da minha existência inteira" (Now, the substance of the benefit was immense, no less than the salvation or the shipwreck of my entire existence—chap. 20). Even as a "casmurro" he recognizes the transporting power of love. His counsel to young men resounds like a battle cry from one who knows by experience what is the most effective weapon: "Amai, rapazes! e, principalmente, amai moças lindas e graciosas; elas dão remédio ao mal, aroma

ao infecto, trocam a morte pela vida ... Amai, rapazes!" (Love,
lads! and, above all, love beautiful, spirited girls. They have a
remedy for ills, fragrance to sweeten a stench; for death they
give you life ... Love, lads, love!—chap. 86). Loving, then is a
weapon against "o naufrágio" and "a morte."

Procreation

Procreation, a logical extension of the concept of love between a man and a woman, is an extremely important matter
for Bentinho. Here we find another correspondence with the
primitive mentality and its rites of fertility. For the primitives,
procreation signified a recreation of themselves, an act of
repetition assuring a sort of immortality. Its absence meant not
only a collective extirpation but also an individual annihilation since the individual saw himself as inseparable from the
community.

In the novel there are moments when Bentinho profoundly
senses the possibility of being childless. At these times we see
through his eyes the image of time as a devouring force. The
occasion of the "duelo de ironias" (duel of ironies), in which
Capitu threatens to find another father for her future son, is a
good example. Bentinho says of the experience:

> Percorreu-me um fluido. Aquela ameaça de um primeiro filho, o
> primeiro filho de Capitu, o casamento dela com outro, portanto, a
> separação absoluta, a perda, a aniquilação, tudo isso produzia um
> tal efeito, que não achei palavra nem gesto; fiquei estúpido.
> Capitu sorria; eu via o primeiro filho brincando no chão.

> I felt a fluid course through me. That threat of a first child,
> Capitu's first child, her marriage with another, absolute separa-
> tion, loss, annihilation, all this so wrought on me that I found
> neither word nor gesture, but sat stupefied. Capitu smiled; I saw
> her first-born playing on the ground. (chap. 45)

Obviously time is not explicitly mentioned here; nevertheless,
it is present as a sort of underlying ogre, ready to eradicate our
hero. Bentinho sees here a double jeopardy: on the one hand,
he finds himself liable to lose Capitu, something that to him
would mean "separação absoluta." We cannot deny the importance he places upon feeling oneness with his beloved, for as we
have seen, it is one of his ways of combatting time. But
besides that abyss of separation, there is the danger of going
through life without posterity. The combination of these

threats accounts for the fact that Bentinho, imagining Capitu's child by another man, sees his own "aniquilação" and is rendered "estúpido."

Taking other comments into account, we further verify the connection between procreation and immortality in Bentinho's mind. Before Ezequiel's birth, Bentinho has an intense longing for a child. He confesses to Escobar that he wants a child for "Uma criança, um filho é o complemento natural da vida" (A child, one's own child, is the natural complement of life—chap. 104), and he even prays for offspring. When Ezequiel is born, Bentinho admits to an indescribable joy, saying that he is "inteiramente nele" (entirely wrapped up in him—chap. 108). After deciding that Ezequiel is not his son, Bentinho still cannot cease to think of him as a weapon against time and death. However, rather than connecting Ezequiel with his own immortality, he associates him with Escobar's. Facing the boy, he says that he sees "Escobar . . . surgindo da sepultura" (Escobar . . . emerging from the grave—chap. 132). Even many years later, upon seeing Ezequiel again, he affirms that he "não gostava da ressurreição" (did not enjoy the resurrection) of his father (chap. 135).

Although it is never easy for a man to reach the conclusion that his wife and child are not really his, for Bentinho this conclusion is uniquely devastating because, as we have seen, in loving communion and procreation he envisions the chance to assure his own existence against the effects of time. Bentinho naturally goes through a period of considerable anguish before definitely deciding that Capitu has been unfaithful. The decision is particularly disagreeable for him since it implies the annihilation of his being. As we saw before, love and procreation for Bentinho were a question of "salvação ou naufrágio." We now note that Santiago narrates that part of his life "como um marujo contaria o seu naufrágio" (as an old sailor recalls his shipwreck—chap. 132).

As I mentioned in chapter 1, there is a metonymy involved in the idea of combatting time through one's progeny. In a literal sense, Bentinho will surely perish like other mortals. But he desires to transfer his identity to someone contiguous—to his offspring. The survival of succeeding generations will be his own victory against time and mortality. Here is another case where the concrete struggle of the mythic hero is transferred and removed from the actual circumstances of a modern protagonist. The myth is retained in a figurative sense but has vanished from the literal account.

Ritual

Having exhausted the resources for transcendence already discussed, Bentinho enters a long phase of "casmurrice." This lack of dynamism corresponds to the death of the mythic hero, who seems to have been destroyed in the battle against the dragon. Nevertheless, Bentinho does not remain entirely defeated because another means of combat still exists for him. I refer here to ritualistic behavior. Through rites—acts of observance that repeat transcendent moments—Bento takes up arms once more against the temporal monster.

We may detect several characteristics of ritual in Bentinho's conduct. Ritual is impractical behavior, in a materialistic sense; hence, we often observe a connection between rite and play. It is something that ought to be repeated. For that reason, there is a formal aspect that must be respected and preserved. Ritual frequently assumes the meaning of a return to the origin, to the moment of initiation or creation. It has a dramatic aspect in which its participants take on the role of other persons, and, generally, it is a collective experience or one of unifying participation among beings.[7]

Even as a young boy Bentinho shows a predisposition toward ritual as a means of fixing time. Let us examine, in this context, the exaggerated importance Bentinho gives to the coconut vendor's street cry. An understanding of the extraordinary meaning Bentinho attaches to the vendor's call is accessible if we recognize that it is associated with a ritualistic act, a dramatization of a crucial prior moment. As I have pointed out, communion with his beloved is a powerful, transporting experience for Bentinho, possessing the capacity to erase, if but for an instant, the perception of worldly time. As a child, Bentinho repeatedly had experiences of "communion" with Capitu, playing "mass": "Em casa, brincava de missa às escondidas, porque minha mãe dizia que missa não era coisa de brincadeira. Arranjávamos um altar, Capitu e eu. Ela servia de sacristão, e alternávamos o ritual, no sentido de dividirmos a hóstia entre nós; hóstia era sempre um doce" (At home, I played Mass—somewhat on the sly, because my mother said that Mass was not a matter for play. We would arrange an altar, Capitu and I. She acted as sacristan and we altered the ritual in the sense that we divided the host between us; the host was always a sweet—chap. 11). It is easy to see the ritual character of this activity. Playing mass was a repetitive act with a formal element that was to be followed to the letter. A necessary element in this formality was the candy.

Although this rite may have been a mere children's game, through time it apparently came to be a true communion, not exactly religious, but always with religious connotations. When as a young man Bentinho feels love's blossoming and experiences a moment of romantic communion, he relies upon the vocabulary of his old priestly play to describe it: "Padre futuro, estava assim diante dela como de um altar, sendo uma das faces a Epístola e a outra o Evangelho. A boca podia ser o cálix, os lábios a pátena. Faltava dizer a missa nova, por um latim que ninguém aprende, e é a língua católica dos homens" (I, future padre, thus stood before her as before an altar, and one side of her face was the Epistle and the other the Gospel. Her mouth the chalice, her lips the paten. It only remained to say the new Mass, in a Latin that no one learns, and that is the catholic language of men—chap. 14). This is another of those profound instants of transcendence. Without pronouncing a single word, with their eyes they say "coisas infinitas" (infinite things—chap. 14). The metaphoric employment of liturgical vocabulary in the description of this encounter connects it with the games mentioned.

Later, Capitu and Bentinho find themselves in danger of being separated. While they discuss the problem, a coconut candy vendor passes, singing his customary street-call, and Bentinho buys two candies. Since candy has been "a host" for them, we can detect a profound dimension in the seemingly banal act of buying a couple of coconut candies and offering one to Capitu. With this, Bentinho wants to partake of the host—to reestablish the communion that existed on other occasions.

It is crucial that rites be repeatable. The sense of repetition or observance of something *in illo tempore* is what gives to the participants the impression of having escaped chronological time. In the case of the candies, we note that Bentinho retains this perception of a crucial, repetitive act. Several years later, he asks Capitu to play the vendor's song on the piano for Ezequiel. When she admits to remembering neither the words nor the notes, Bentinho finds among his old papers a transcription of the chant, which he had requested from a music professor (chap. 110). Bentinho says he had made a mutual promise with Capitu never to forget the song—a promise only he seems to have remembered (chap. 114). Evidently, there is in his mind a subtle link between the song and the candy and between the candy and a few very sweet moments of union between souls. Remembering and reproducing the song, he unconsciously seems to want to depart from present time and return to that beginning when two children communed.

As an adult, the narrator displays the same ritualistic behavior, seeking to erase the sense of linear time. Donaldo Schüler mentions a notable case in point,[8] the reproduction of his boyhood home. In an attitude in which "tudo [lhe] era estranho e adverso" (it was all strange and hostile—chap. 144), he let the demolition crew do away with the original house on Rua Matacavalos. Years later, he has an identical version built in Engenho Novo. Note his preoccupation with the formal aspect of the reproduction:

> Construtor e pintor entenderam bem as indicações que lhes fiz: é o mesmo prédio assobradado, três janelas de frente, varanda ao fundo, as mesmas alcovas e salas. Na principal destas, a pintura do teto e das paredes é mais ou menos igual, umas grinaldas de flores miúdas e grandes pássaros que as tomam nos bicos, de espaço a espaço. Nos quatro cantos do teto as figuras das estações, e ao centro das paredes os medalhões de César, Augusto, Nero e Massinissa, com os nomes por baixo.

> Builder and decorator understood my instructions. It is the same tall structure with three windows across the front, veranda at the back, the same rooms upstairs and down. In the living room, the decoration of ceiling and walls is more or less identical: garlands of tiny flowers steadied, from space to space, by the beaks of stout birds. In the four corners of the ceiling, are the figures of the seasons; and in the center of the walls, the medallions of Caesar, Augustus, Nero and Massinissa, with their names beneath. (chap. 2)

This exact duplication is without logic in the obvious context in which a house is a shelter against bad weather, or "mau tempo." The narrator himself admits that he does not know "a razão dos medalhões" (the reason for the medallions—chap. 2). In the context of primitive thought, however, that conspicuous formality does have its logic, for it is all part of a construction of another type of protection against "tempo"—not against atmospheric upheavals but against the destructive flood of the clock. Recreating the old house detail for detail, Bento seeks to detach himself from linear time and become immersed in a cyclical time. When the narrator says that his objective in constructing the house "era atar as duas pontas da vida" (was to tie together the two ends of my life—chap. 2), he chooses a very propitious metaphor to contrast profane time and mythic time. The "profane" is rigidly linear; it has a beginning, middle, and end, and the two extremities are inseparable. The mythic, on the other hand, is cyclical and repeatable; beginning and finality can be tied like the two ends of a piece of twine.

In the attempt to abolish time, Santiago's act of writing memoirs is still another sort of ritual effort. Each narration, fictional or authentic, is by definition the observance of a prior event. The narrator *represents* something, or in other words, makes something present again that was present before. Naturally, what Bento Santiago wants to make present in writing is the enchantment of a star-struck adolescent. Meditating upon his slight success in reviving old times by means of the rebuilt house, he discovers another idea:

> Foi então que os bustos pintados nas paredes entraram a falar-me que, uma vez que eles não alcançaram reconstituir-me os tempos idos, pegasse da pena e contasse alguns. Talvez a narração me desse a ilusão, e as sombras viessem perpassar ligeiras, como ao poeta . . . de *Fausto: Aí vindes outra vez, inquietas sombras?* . . . Deste modo, viverei o que vivi. . . .

> It was then that the busts painted on the walls spoke to me and said that since they had failed to bring back the days gone by, I should take my pen and tell over those times. Perhaps the act of narration would summon the illusion for me, and the shades would come treading lightly, as with the poet . . . in *Faust: Ah there, are you come again restless shades?* . . . In this way I will live what I have lived. . . . (chap. 2)

The reconstruction of the house and the narration are, then, parallel acts. Both are designed to "atar as duas pontas da vida." When Bento says that, writing, "viverei o que vivi," he clearly exposes his goal; in a grammatical sense, he is already trying to tie together the past and future tenses.

Modernity and Dis-Illusionment

The connection between house and book, and the ritual function of both, are elucidated in chapter 64, entitled "Uma idéia e um escrúpulo" (An idea and a scruple). Here a third element, a remembered dream, serves as an intermediary in the comparison between writing and constructing a replica of the house. In the preceding chapter Bento relates that while in the seminary, he dreamt about an encounter with Capitu. The atmosphere in the dream was like that of the hair-combing session; Capitu was beholding him tenderly and seemed to promise a kiss. However, Bentinho awoke before the kiss and spent the rest of the night trying to reestablish the interrupted dream.

The awakening from a dream is a moment of disillusionment—in the common sense of disappointment but also in the stricter sense of "loss of illusion." Waking up abruptly in the middle of a delicious dream, Bentinho feels despair upon realizing that he is in the seminary and not in Capitu's arms. His disillusion is truly a "dis-illusion."

The interrupted dream is a model through which the acts of writing memoirs and of rebuilding old houses are compared. In both cases there is also an awakening from a sort of dream, or a "dis-illusion." The narrator looks at the walls of his office and recognizes that he is not in the old, authentic house but rather in its reproduction: "Deixei o manuscrito, e olhei para as paredes. Sabes que esta casa do Engenho Novo . . . é a reprod-ução da minha antiga casa de Matacavalos" (I turned away from the manuscript and looked at the walls. You know that this house in Engenho Novo . . . is the reproduction of my old Matacavalos house—chap. 64). Although it may be possible at times to delude himself into thinking he is in the old house, it is not possible now. The narrator becomes acutely conscious that his narration is not life relived but writing. We find here images of the machinery of composition. Chapters are mentioned various times (one even by number), and the author stares at his manuscript. Santiago had said upon beginning the book, "Talvez a narração me desse a ilusão" (Perhaps the act of narration would summon the illusion) of living in the past again. At the narration of this chapter, it becomes more than clear to him that the "ilusão" he longed for is just that—mere illusion.

Reflecting again upon the interrupted dream, the narrator concludes:

> . . . Como te disse no capítulo II, o meu fim em imitar a outra [casa] foi ligar as duas pontas da vida, o que aliás não alcancei. Pois o mesmo sucedeu àquele sonho do seminário, por mais que

tentasse dormir e dormisse. Donde concluo que um dos ofícios do homem é fechar e apertar muito os olhos, e ver se continua pela noite velha o sonho truncado na noite moca.

. . . as I told you in Chapter 2, my purpose in recreating the other house was to link together the two ends of my life, which, by the way, I have not accomplished. Well, the same thing happened to that dream at the seminary, no matter how much I tried to sleep and did sleep. From this I conclude that one of the offices of man is to close his eyes and hold them tight shut to see if the dream that was interrupted when the night was young will continue through the dead hours. (chap. 64)

Both the rebuilding of the house and the narration, therefore, have a ritualistic purpose: to continue "pela noite velha o sonho truncado na noite moça." But just as the seminary dreamer does not manage to continue the dream, the mature man's ritualistic behavior does not entirely succeed in reproducing the earlier sensations. It is always a repetition, a mediated version of an original and immediate essence.

In the same chapter Bento laments the fact that the "old dreams" do not exist any more. He now seems to be using the word "sonho" in the more abstract sense of "fantasy" or "profound desire." He says that in olden times dreams

moravam na ilha que Luciano lhes deu, onde [a noite] tinha o seu palácio, e donde os fazia sair com suas caras de vária feição. . . . Mas os tempos mudaram tudo. Os sonhos antigos foram aposentados, e os modernos moram no cérebro da pessoa. Estes, ainda que quisessem imitar os outros, não poderiam fazê-lo; a ilha dos sonhos, como a dos amores, como todas as ilhas de todos os mares, são agora objeto da ambição e da rivalidade de Europa e dos Estados Unidos.

dwelt on the island that Lucian had given them, where [the night] had her palace, and from whence she sent them forth with their faces of divers aspect. . . . But the times have changed everything. The ancient dreams have been retired, and the modern ones dwell in a person's brain. And these, though they might try to imitate the former, could not do it: the isle of dreams, like the isle of love, and all the islands of all the seas, are now the object of the ambition and rivalry of Europe and the United States. (chap. 64)

Here is the lament of a primitive mind, bound to modernity, as well as a good summary of Bentinho's main problem insofar as time is concerned. In the passage there is a dichotomy between ancient dreams or desires, that were part of a mythic territory (the "palácio da ilha dos sonhos"), and modern dreams, whose territory is the object of political disputes between modern nations. He establishes here a contrast between a mythic existence, heroic and primitive, and a modern existence based upon material preoccupations. Bentinho's dream is to escape modern time in order to attain mythic time. In a very few cases, through love, he succeeds in effecting this transportation. But normally he remains caged in the present, a victim of retired dreams, trying in vain to reconnect with the beginnings.

The last words of the book, "Vamos à *História dos Subúrbios*" (On to the *History of the Suburbs*—Chap. 148), are a disillusioned recognition in Bento that his mythic personality, the part that fights the dragon of time, cannot but fail. No matter how much he tries, Dom Casmurro cannot belong to the Isle of Dreams. On the contrary, he must belong to the suburbs—to the region of third-party judicial proceedings, trains from the Central Station to Engenho Novo, and interim administrations.

CHAPTER THREE

Birth, Death, and Rebirth

Having identified time as the nemesis of Bentinho, our "hero," we should recognize that the enemy so conceptualized is a mental construction, an abstraction that exists as a by-product of more sensible and fundamental phenomena.[1] Time is grounded in concrete experience with its perpetual rhythm of change. Those most basic events of life—inhaling and exhaling, waking and sleeping, being born and dying—give time its reality and importance. If time is indeed such a central factor in the novel, we should expect to be able to examine a more tangible system of images underlying the experience of time, involving many cyclical processes of life.

Under the rubric of the so-called "rebirth pattern" or "rebirth archetype," this chapter will analyze that sort of dimension in *Dom Casmurro*. This approach will permit us to understand how numerous images and motifs in the novel, mainly involving the physical and emotional state of Bentinho, provide concrete grounding for his anti-temporal quest.

Any motif involving the restoration of life may be called a manifestation of the rebirth archetype. "Restoration" implies prior plenitude and loss. The rebirth pattern thus involves a three-part sequence: vitality, loss of vitality, recuperation of vitality. This cyclical process harmonizes with another important triad—the separation, initiation, and return of the quest myth. The two patterns correspond in various ways. Given the fact that in the quest myth separation practically always implies some necessity (shortage, loss), we can say that both the rebirth pattern and the quest are restorative. As I mentioned in chapter 1, Northrop Frye considers the quest myth to be analogous to the yearly cycle (which is a rebirth pattern).[2] They also harmonize in that both patterns end where they began. This isomorphism permits a variety of displaced, metaphoric versions of the quest and allows us to find traces of the quest in episodes, including many in *Dom Casmurro*, in which the heroic element is far from apparent.

A Tidal Rhythm

Maud Bodkin has called the rebirth motif "the tidal ebb toward death followed by life renewal, [which] affords us a means of increased awareness, and of fuller expression and control, of our lives in their secret and momentous obedience to universal rhythms."[3] The comparison she suggests between the tide, with its slow, steady, and unchangeable rhythm, and the death-birth pattern is especially appropriate for discussing Machado's novel because of the importance of tidal imagery involving the word "ressaca."

One of the definitions for that richly ambiguous word is "fluxo e refluxo" (tidal ebb and flow), according to the *Pequeno dicionário brasileiro da língua portuguesa*. The word also denotes the meaning of the English word "undertow." Just as Capitu's "olhos de ressaca" (undertow eyes) have the power to sweep in Bentinho, and just as Flamengo's "ressaca" takes control of Escobar and pulls him under its waves, the image of the "ressaca" seems to be able to sweep in the entire work, for the novel becomes subject to a tide-like cadence of rising and falling emotion, a kind of "secret and momentous obedience to universal rhythms" of time and life.

Metaphoric Dimensions

The rebirth pattern may manifest itself in several ways within various domains of imagery. Some common types of patterns are (1) emotional: frustration followed by resolution, (2) dynamic: stoppage and restoration of energy flow, (3) communicative: reticence followed by fluency, (4) luminary: darkness followed by light, (5) spatial: departure from confined surroundings, (6) aqueous: emergence from moisture, and (7) representational: recreation through narrative, ritual, or drama.[4]

In all of these domains, the change from inertia to vitality is normally beyond the power of those involved, suggesting the spontaneity of the onset of birth. For example, there is a long tradition of narrators such as the Ancient Mariner, the Wandering Jew, and the Flying Dutchman, who go about telling their stories *by compulsion* to anyone who will listen. In effect, these narrators are pregnant with their tales and do not have complete control over the time of circumstances in which the stories are "born." If the narrator has strong power of determination over his tale, he does not participate in this aspect of the rebirth pattern. *Dom Casmurro*'s narrator attempts to participate in this type of rebirth by telling his story. That narrative reliving, however, is marginal to the novel's actual plot. In addition, as chapter 2 brings out, it is an ironic reliving at best.

Rebirth and the Novel's Plot Structure

To see the overall form of the rebirth archetype as it appears in *Dom Casmurro*, it helps to "step back" from the narrative, forget about details, and capsulize as if we were giving a thirty-second plot summary. As I will show later in detail, the birth-death rhythm in the life of Bentinho corresponds to the following rising and falling action of the plot: birth—Bentinho falls in love; death—Bentinho enters the seminary; birth—Bentinho leaves the seminary and marries; death—Bentinho is convinced that his wife has been unfaithful. Figure 3.1 gives a graphic representation of the pattern:[5]

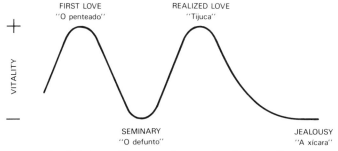

Fig. 3.1: Dom Casmurro's *overall rebirth pattern*

The line traces Bentinho's process of "birth" and "death" through time. The words in capital letters refer to the outward signs of each phase. Those in quotation marks refer to key images which occur when the birth or death processes seem to culminate. Bentinho's story begins in the chapter entitled "A denúncia" (The information). It is particularly interesting to notice the physical setting established in that chapter. The narrator says, "Ia a entrar na sala de visitas, quando ouvi proferir meu nome e escondi-me atrás da porta" (I was about to go into the living room when I heard my name mentioned and hid behind the door—chap. 3). Four persons are present in the "sala de visitas." However, the dominant person in the room is D. Glória, Bentinho's mother, for all of the remarks of José Dias, Prima Justina, and Tio Cosme center around her plan to "meter o nosso Bentinho no seminário" (put our Bentinho in the seminary—chap. 3). Bentinho would presumably have entered the room without a second thought under other circumstances, but when he hears his name, he senses that an important conversation about him is taking place, and he is "expelled," as it were, from the room. He remains listening in the hallway, behind a door.

The spatial situation here is a birth metaphor. We see Bentinho being pushed out of a mother's chamber. The placement of the mother inside this womb-like space, instead of vice versa, is a transformation through synecdoche of the normal phenomenon. However, it is still appropriate to identify the "sala de visitas" as a maternal space. Outside this chamber Bentinho is "trapped" in the hallway—a narrow passageway, by extension suggestive of the birth canal. The fact that he is behind the door increases the impression of his being closed in but about to be freed.

After several digressive expository chapters, Bentinho does leave the corridor: "Tão depressa vi desaparecer o agregado no corredor, deixei o esconderijo, e corri à varanda do fundo" (As soon as I saw our dependent disappear down the hall, I left my hiding place and ran to the veranda at the back—chap. 11). His passage from the chamber to the hallway hiding place to the outdoor veranda continues the suggested birth process. In retrospect, the narrator confirms that those decisive moments were similar to being born: "Verdadeiramente foi o princípio da minha vida; tudo o que sucedera antes foi como o pintar e vestir das pessoas que tinham de entrar em cena, o acender das luzes, o preparar das rabecas, a sinfonia... Agora é que ia começar a minha ópera" (Actually it was the beginning of my life; all that had gone before was like the making-up and costuming of those about to go on stage, like the turning up of the lights, the tuning of the fiddles, the overture... Now I was to commence my opera—chap. 8).

Once Bentinho runs to the veranda, he seems overcome with "um gozo novo" (a new sensation), as if he were feeling the first breath of life: "Esse primeiro palpitar da seiva, essa revelação da consciência a si própria, nunca mais me esqueceu, nem achei que lhe fosse comparável qualquer outra sensação da mesma espécie, naturalmente por ser minha. Naturalmente também por ser a primeira" (This first pulsating of sap, this revelation of consciousness to itself—I have never forgotten it. I have never known any similar sensation to compare with it. Probably because it was mine; probably also because it was the first—chap. 12).

Describing his legs at this moment, Bento gives the impression of an infant learning to walk. At first they are "as pernas bambas" (wobbly legs—chap. 12), which seem hardly able to support his weight. Later they are more sure of themselves: "E as minhas pernas andavam, desandavam, estancavam, trêmulas e crentes de abarcar o mundo" (And my legs walked to and fro, they halted, quivering, eager to bestride the world—chap. 12). Still later they are even steadier; he calls them "andarilhas" (robust—chap. 13).

What brings on this rebirth, of course, is Bentinho's discovery that he is in love with Capitu. José Dias' suggestion to D. Glória of romantic inclinations between Bentinho and Capitu causes a serendipitous recognition of that truth within the boy.

As the preceding figure shows, the metaphoric "birth" is not an isolated event but rather the beginning of a process extending over a considerable period of time. The process reaches its culmination in the episode of the combing, in which Bentinho and Capitu mutually express their love.

In the last chapter I discussed this episode at some length as an example of a moment when Bentinho succeeds in annihilating his perception of chronological time. The connection between the defeat of time and the culmination of a sort of birth seems particularly appropriate if we remember that time and mortality are intimately connected. It seems logical that the rebirth archetype, that universal symbol of immortality, should often involve the eradication of time. We will see that the same temporal transcendence appears at the culmination of the next rebirth phase as well.

A short time after the grooming session, Bentinho declares, "Sou homem!" (I am a man!—chap. 34), perhaps unconsciously acknowledging that the first vital stage of his life has reached its fruition. He has been born into love, he has been a toddler, an insecure child, and now he has matured.

After the momentous kiss, Capitu undoes Bentinho's hair-do. Likewise, from that point onward for several chapters, Bentinho's hopes for fulfillment are gradually undone. Little by little, ambiguous challenging actions on the part of Capitu, Bentinho's inability to go against his mother's wishes, and the first signs of his jealousy cause a dark cloud to form, blocking out the rays of hope.

It is appropriate that this frustration or downward action in the plot coincides with Bentinho's entry into the seminary, for the seminary, with its cloistered, isolated quality is spatially suggestive of the grave or the mother's womb. Just as Jonah enters the belly of the whale, remains there in a moribund state for awhile, and then is spewed out, endowed with renewed vigor, so Machado's protagonist enters the walled-in seminary and experiences a loss of self-asserting power before being suddenly delivered with a new sense of hope and dynamism.

It is helpful to remember that the seminary, like the living room, is in a way Bentinho's mother's territory. Bentinho's presence in the seminary is solely in obedience to D. Glória's will and not through any sense of vocation. This fact further strengthens the seminary's symbolic association with the womb by a sort of metonymy of influence.

Several factors accentuate the connotations of the seminary as a place of lifelessness. Artistic juices do not seem to flow within the atmosphere of the seminary. For example, Bentinho tries to compose a sonnet, but succeeds in supplying only the first and last lines: "Oh! flor do céu! oh! flor cândida e pura!" and "Perde-se a vida, ganha-se a batalha" (O flower of heaven! O flower bright and pure; Life is lost, the battle still is won—chap. 55). We notice that the first line contains images of life, not to mention no fewer than four exclamation points, while the last contains images of death. So it is with Bentinho's artistic urge. What begins with vitality, ends with frustration. Obviously, Bentinho recuperates his ability to write in later life. However, the seminary and its extension, the priesthood, seem to have killed the artistic ability of a former colleague who used to write verses while in the seminary, who went on to become a priest, and who quit writing poetry (chap. 54).

It is at the seminary that Bentinho first seriously doubts whether Capitu will keep her vow to marry him. José Dias awakens these doubts when he jokingly remarks during a visit about the possibility of her being claimed in matrimony by some "peralta da vizinhança" (young buck of the neighborhood—chap. 62).

While Bentinho is at the seminary, D. Glória becomes very sick. As Bentinho walks home with José Dias to see his mother, he is again stricken with a case of "pernas bambas" (wobbly legs). This perhaps signifies a metaphoric return to the helplessness of infancy. He says at this time, "Era a primeira vez que a morte me aparecia assim perto, me envolvia, me encarava com os olhos furados e escuros" (It was the first time that death had come close to me, enveloping me, peering into my face with its dim sunken eyes—chap. 67). On the way, he is struck with that "ruim pensamento" (wicked thought), "Mamãe dufunta, acaba o seminário" (With Mamma dead, that would be the end of the seminary—chap. 67), about which the narrator remarks, "Leitor, foi um relâmpago. Tão depressa alumiou a noite, como se esvaiu, e a escuridão fez-se mais cerrada" (Reader, it was a lightning flash; no sooner had it illuminated the night than it fled away, leaving the dark more intense—chap. 67). Through his momentary selfish death-wish, Bentinho becomes locked for some time inside a "noite cerrada" of guilt feelings.

Also during his seminary career, Bentinho is confronted with the horrifying face of his acquaintance, Manduca, who has just died from leprosy. While walking along the street, Bentinho is called in by Manduca's father to take a look at the boy. He enters the family's residence, a small store: "A loja era escura, e o interior da casa menos luz tinha, agora que as janelas da área estavam cerradas. A um canto da sala de jantar vi a mãe chorando; à porta da alcova duas crianças olhavam espantadas para dentro, com o dedo na boca. O cadáver jazia na cama" (The shop was dim and the inside of the house had less light now that the windows on the court were darkened. I saw the mother crying in a corner of the dining room. At the bedroom door, two children stared inside in frightened wonder, finger in mouth. The corpse lay on the bed—chap. 85).

Bentinho steps inside the bedroom and looks at Manduca's disfigured face: "Vivo era feio; morto pareceu-me horrível. Quando eu vi, estendido na cama, o triste corpo daquele meu vizinho, fiquei apavorado e desviei os olhos. Não sei que mão oculta me compeliu a olhar outra vez, ainda que de fugida; cedi, olhei, tornei a olhar, até que recuei de todo e saí do quarto" (In life he was ugly; in death he seemed horrible. When I saw him stretched out on the bed, the pitiful body of him who had been my neighbor, I was horrified, and turned away my eyes. I do not know what unseen hand compelled me to look a second time, even fleetingly; I yielded, I looked, kept looking, until I backed away completely and left the room—chap. 85).

Bentinho's entrance into the dark, closed-in atmosphere of the store, and his further entrance into Manduca's bedroom to encounter the disfigured body, is a metaphoric capsulization of the archetypal hero's struggle with death—a variation of the entry into a dragon's cave or into the belly of a whale. This episode seems to mark the low point in the narrative's swing between life and death. Bentinho's stay within the walls of the seminary is in a way too diffuse to represent the death phase of the rebirth pattern. Although symbolically the seminary can be associated with the grave or the mother's womb, its treatment within the novel covers too much time and contains too many digressions to provide a concentrated effect. Bentinho's seminary experience, after all, covers forty-four chapters or almost one third of the space of the novel. Besides that, Machado devotes much more attention to Bentinho's weekend visits at home during this time than to his seminary experience. The Manduca episode is what might be called a "free motif," or one that could be removed entirely from the novel and not destroy the causality of the plot.[6] However, the episode has an important part to play as a metonymic intensifier in the emotional cycle of the novel, accompanying the ebb and flow of the rebirth rhythm. The suggestiveness of entrance into and reemergence from the seminary as a bout with death is in effect diluted in the narrative because of the need to include other elements in the plot. There is a need to fortify it somehow. What appears to have satisfied that supposed emotional need is the Manduca episode with its terrifying glimpse of death. Once the emotional intensity is restored to the deathward ebb, the narrative is ready to begin the flow toward life once more. It only takes a few more chapters until Bentinho leaves the seminary once and for all.

By means of Escobar's plan for an orphan substitute (reminiscent perhaps of the scapegoat motif so common in myth), Bentinho passes through the seminary gates that once seemed so constraining into the outside world of liberty and love. Appropriately, he is "born" into the outside world through no effort of his own. Before we know it, he has completed law school and is ready to marry Capitu. As he prepares for the ceremony, the voice of an imaginary fairy assures him, "Tu serás feliz" (You will be happy—chap. 100).

Bentinho's marriage completes his rebirth. He mentions that it rained on his wedding day (chap. 101). Rain, an image suggesting the release of energy, reinforces the notion of rebirth.[7]

The apex of the process seems to be the week-long honeymoon at the "alto da Tijuca" (Tijuca hilltop). The name's suggested altitude is significant, for it conforms to a traditional set of images of the "point of epiphany," the place where the heaven and earth meet.[8] The chapter describing the marriage also implies epiphany with its title—"No céu" (In heaven—chap. 101). Still another image suggesting the culmination of rebirth, or epiphany, is the bright, starry sky that reveals itself after the rain: "O céu recolheu a chuva e acendeu as estrelas, não só as já conhecidas, mas ainda as que só serão descobertas daqui a muitos séculos" (The sky held back the rain and lighted the stars, not only those already known but also ones which will not be discovered until many centuries from now—chap. 101). As in the other culminating episode, "O penteado" (The combing), the narrator describes the transition of the element of time from the terrestrial realm into an eternal realm. Before, unending strands of hair suggested eternity; now the image employed is a clock without a pendulum (see chapter 2).

The Tijuca honeymoon, like any other, must unavoidably end. In the novel it ends with a descent from the mountain into the city. The physical shift from height to depth corresponds with a gradual emotional descent into the depths of frustration and despair.

Northrop Frye discusses types of imagery frequently associated with the tragic phase of the quest myth or the symbolic death of the hero. He mentions images of the ocean, of floods, and of water monsters as being typical of the phase's "unformed world": "Water . . . traditionally belongs to the realm of existence below human life, the state of chaos or dissolution which follows ordinary death, or the reduction to the inorganic."[9]

In the final phase of the story of Capitu and Bentinho, aquatic imagery takes on increased importance. And in the case of *Dom Casmurro*, this water imagery indeed suggests the "chaos" and "dissolution" Frye refers to. The phase's first instance of powerful water imagery occurs one night when Bentinho is trying to give Capitu an astronomy lesson. Bentinho is disturbed when he discovers that she has not been accompanying him in his celestial gazing: ". . . perdeu-se em fitar o mar, com tal força que me deu ciúmes" (. . . she was so lost in contemplation of the sea, it made me jealous—chap. 106). Capitu's wandering eyes—in themselves imbued with the powerful aqueous suggestiveness of the undertow—had strayed earlier to a young man passing on horseback; Bentinho became jealous of the passing "dandy." Now they have wandered to the sea, and Bentinho, realizing that he does not have complete possession of his wife, feels jealous once again.

As Bentinho's suspicion grows and takes control of him, the sea imagery in the novel also grows and, in a sense, takes control of the emotional tone. Especially worthy of note is the tumultuous chapter, "A mão de Sancha" (The hand of Sancha), in which Bentinho perceives that Escobar's wife is flirting with him. The nature imagery outdoors accompanies the unsteadiness of the relationships depicted inside:

> O mar batia com grande força na praia; havia ressaca.
>
> . . . . .
>
> —O mar amanhã está de desafiar a gente, disse-me a voz de Escobar, ao pé de mim.
>
> —Você entra no mar amanhã?
>
> —Tenho entrado com mares maiores, muito maiores. Você não imagina o que é um bom mar em hora bravia.
>
> . . . . .
>
> Ouvia-se o mar forte—como já se ouvia de casa,—a ressaca era grande, e, à distância, viam-se crescer as ondas.
>
> The sea pounded forcibly along the shore; and there was the suck of the undertow.

. . . . .

"Tomorrow, the sea will be a challenge," it was the voice of Escobar, who was standing at my side.

"You intend to swim in that sea tomorrow?"

"I've gone in in worse, much worse. You can't imagine what a good wild sea is like."

. . . . .

We heard the roar of the sea—as we had heard it from the house—the undertow was strong, and in the distance we could see the waves rise in great swells. (chap. 118)

As the narrator points out in chapter 119, the story reaches the edge of an abyss. The plunge into the emotional abyss occurs when the "ressaca" claims Escobar's life. The important image of Capitu's "olhos de ressaca" enters the narrative with powerful force as Capitu views Escobar's body at the wake:

A confusão era geral. No meio dela, Capitu olhou alguns instantes para o cadáver tão fixa, tão apaixonadamente fixa, que não admira lhe saltassem algumas lágrimas poucas e caladas...

As minhas cessaram logo. Fiquei a ver as dela; Capitu enxugou-as depressa, olhando a furto para a gente que estava na sala. Redobrou de carícias para a amiga, e quis levá-la; mas o cadáver parece que a retinha também. Momento houve em que os olhos de Capitu fitaram o defunto, quais os da viúva, sem o pranto nem palavras desta, mas grandes e abertos, como a vaga do mar lá fora, como se quisesse tragar também o nadador da manhã.

The consternation was general. In the midst of it, Capitu gazed down for a few seconds at the corpse, gazed so fixedly, with such passionate fixedness, that it was no wonder if tears sprang to her eyes, a few, quiet tears...

My own ceased at once. I stood looking at hers; she wiped them away in haste, glancing furtively around at the people in the room. She redoubled her caresses to her friend, and tried to take her away, but the corpse seemed to hold her too. There was a moment when Capitu's eyes gazed down at the dead man just as the widow's had, though without her weeping or any accompanying words, but great and wide like the swollen wave of the sea beyond, as if she too wished to swallow up the swimmer of that morning. (chap. 123)

The image of the "ressaca," with its suggestiveness of the violent thrashing of the sea, thus becomes the unifying image for all the forces that bring about Bentinho's descent from vitality to the depths of "casmurrice." The "ressaca" sweeps away Bentinho's best friend. Bentinho's examination of his wife's eyes as they look at Escobar's body causes him to suspect that her "olhos de ressaca" have likewise swept in Escobar.

Before narrating his final jealous encounter with Capitu, the narrator again introduces the imagery of the stormy sea, as if to summarize its metaphorical relationship to his emotional state:

> . . . os nossos temporais eram agora contínuos e terríveis. Antes de descoberta aquela má terra da verdade, tivemos outros de pouca dura; não tardava que o céu se fizesse azul, o sol claro e o mar chão, por onde abríamos novamente as velas que nos levavam às ilhas mais belas do universo, até que outro pé de vento desbaratava tudo, e nós, postos à capa, esperávamos outra bonança, que não era tardia nem dúbia, antes total, próxima e firme.
>
> Relevam-me estas metáforas; cheiram ao mar e à maré que deram morte ao meu amigo e comborço Escobar. Cheiram também aos olhos de ressaca de Capitu. Assim, posto sempre fosse homem de terra, conto aquela parte da minha vida, como um marujo contaria o seu naufrágio.
>
> . . . our storms had now become continuous and terrible. Before discovering that evil land of Truth, we had had other storms, but of short duration—before long the sky would be blue, the sun bright and the sea smooth, and we would again unfurl our sails, and they would carry us to the fairest islands and coasts of the universe until another squall blew down everything, and we lay to, waiting for another calm; it would not be slow in coming, nor would it be doubtful, but rather complete, near at hand, and sure.
>
> Forgive these metaphors; they savor of the sea and of the tide which brought death to my friend, my wife's lover, Escobar. They savor also of Capitu's eyes, eyes like the tide when the undertow is strong. And so, though I have always been a landsman, I tell this part of my life as an old sailor recalls his shipwreck. (chap. 132)

Santiago's conviction that his great love and his greatest friend united to betray him and that they were destined to do so (chap. 148) causes the protagonist to sink into lifelessness. Although he does not literally die, his transformation into an "homem calado e metido consigo," with "hábitos reclusos e calados" (a morose, tight-lipped man withdrawn within himself, with taciturn, recluse-like habits—chap. 1) is a metaphorical death and signals the waning of emotional and spiritual vitality.

Bentinho's attempts to use the poison and his confrontation with Capitu are the darkest moments of the pattern's deathward swing. A number of images of darkness poetically intensify the

mood of death: a fixed idea, which "negrejava" (grew in black-
ness) in Bentinho's mind, an allusion to Shakespeare's dark hero
Othello, and most importantly the poisoned cup of coffee.

As if to sustain the emotional impact of Bento's fall, the
novel narrates the deaths of several other characters in close
sequence. D. Glória, José Dias, Capitu, and Ezequiel all die
within the space of five chapters. Within this same space,
Bento also tells of destroying the house in which he was raised.
The atmosphere is indeed one of dissolution and chaos.[10]

As with the "Manduca" episode in the previous death-like
phase of the narrative, there appears to be an episode inserted
in this part—another "free motif"—that has a very marginal
connection with anything in the story. The purpose of this
motif seems to be to intensify the reader's emotional response
as he accompanies Bentinho in his fall. I refer to the strange
episode in which Bentinho, Escobar, and their families suspend
their activities for a moment to watch a cat kill a mouse:

> Um dia, na chácara de Escobar, [Ezequiel] deu com um gato que
> tinha um rato atravessado na boca. O gato nem deixava a presa, nem
> via por onde fugisse. Ezequiel não disse nada, deteve-se, acocorou-se,
> e ficou olhando. Ao vê-lo assim atento, perguntamos-lhe de longe o
> que era; fez-nos sinal que nos calássemos. Escobar concluiu:
>
> —Vão ver que é o gato que apanhou algum rato. Os ratos
> continuam a infestar-me a casa que é o diabo. Vamos ver.
>
> Capitu quis também ver a filho; acompanhei-os. Efetivamente,
> era um gato e um rato, lance banal, sem interesse nem graça. A
> única circunstância particular era estar o rato vivo, esperneando,
> e o meu pequeno enlevado. De resto, o instante foi curto. O gato,
> logo que sentiu mais gente, dispôs-se a correr; o menino, sem
> tirar-lhe os olhos de cima, fez-nos outro sinal de silêncio; e o
> silêncio não podia ser maior. Ia dizer religioso, risquei a palavra,
> mas aqui a ponho outra vez, não só por significar a totalidade do
> silêncio, mas também porque havia naquela ação do gato e rato
> alguma coisa que prendia com ritual.

One day, at Escobar's place, [Ezequiel] came across a cat with a
mouse in its teeth. The cat would not release its prey and yet did not
know where to run. Ezequiel did not make a sound; he stopped,
crouched, and kept looking. When we saw him so, all intent, we
called to him and asked what it was. He made a sign for us to be quiet.
Escobar surmised, "I'll bet it's the cat and he's caught a mouse. I
can't get rid of the mice in this place; they're the very devil. I'll see."

Capitu also wanted to see what the boy was doing. I went
along. As a matter of fact, it was a cat and a mouse, commonplace

event, without interest or charm. The only peculiar circumstance was that the mouse was alive, kicking, and my little son entranced. But the instant was short. As soon as the cat saw more people, it prepared to run. The child, keeping his eyes on it, again motioned us for silence, and the silence could not have been greater. I was going to say religious; I scratched out the word, but I put it in here once more, not only to signify the totality of the silence but also because there was in the action of the cat and the mouse something akin to ritual. (chap. 110)

Later, the narrator admits that he feels a "simpatia ao rato" (sympathy for the mouse—chap. 111). While the protagonist never suffers physically, he associates himself metaphorically with the agonizing mouse. This device increases the affective weight of his figurative "death."

The Progression-Regression Cycle

As the tide's slow inward and outward motion contains the oscillating movement of many smaller waves, so the overall birth-death wave created in *Dom Casmurro* is accompanied by a rising and falling emotional movement of greater frequency and lesser amplitude. Figure 3.2 graphically portrays these smaller ebbs and swells:

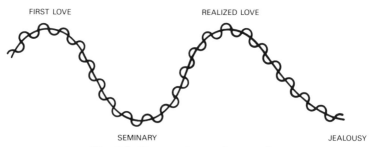

FIRST LOVE   REALIZED LOVE

SEMINARY   JEALOUSY

Fig. 3.2: Progression and regression

This minute wave pattern, which traces the daily flux of Bentinho's psyche, corresponds to what C. G. Jung has called the cycle of progression and regression—a sway between extroversion and introversion, expansive hope and frustration, action and quiescence.[11]

A good example of this process is to be seen soon after José Dias' revelation, when Bentinho and Capitu meet by the backyard wall. Bentinho is about to enter into Capitu's yard:

"Quis passar ao quintal, mas as pernas, há pouco tão andarilhas, pareciam agora presas ao chão. Afinal, fiz um esforço, empurrei a porta, e entrei" (I wanted to go into the yard, but my legs, just now so lively, clung fast to the ground. I made an effort, I shoved the gate and went in—chap. 13). We note that Bentinho, because of frustration or shyness, is for a moment powerless; his legs seem "presas ao chão." His energy to act seems for some reason to be trapped inside him. In a moment, that force begins to flow again: "Afinal, fiz um esforço, empurrei a porta, e entrei." The image of his pushing open a door corresponds with a psychic movement or an unstopping and outward movement of energy. Here is the rebirth pattern seen under a microscope. For an instant, capacity dies. Then that power comes to life and is released with its parallel spirit of hope and expansiveness. We continue now with the young lovers' encounter:

> Caminhei para ela; naturalmente levava o gesto mudado, porque ela veio a mim, e perguntou-me inquieta:
> —Que é que você tem?
> —Eu? Nada.
> —Nada, não; você tem alguma coisa.
> Quis insistir que nada mas não achei língua.

> I walked toward her. Probably I wore a new expression, for she came to me and asked uneasily:
> "What's the matter with you?"
> "With me? Nothing."
> "No, no, there *is* something."
> I wanted to insist that there was nothing, but I could not move my tongue. (chap. 13)

Bentinho's vital energy has again slipped into confinement. The phenomenon manifest here—the incapacity to speak—is extremely frequent in the novel. Bentinho continues for a time in this attitude. Verbs such as "balbuciei" (I stammered) and "emendei" (I corrected myself) indicate frustrated speech. Again Bentinho mentions the problem: "sentir que não poderia falar claramente" (feeling that I could not speak clearly—chap. 13). Capitu then brings Bentinho out of himself by revealing the secret her hand has held concealed—their two names, scratched into the wall:

> Voltei-me para ela; Capitu tinha os olhos no chão. Ergueu-os logo, devagar, e ficamos a olhar um para o outro... Confissão de

crianças, tu valias bem duas ou três páginas, mas quero ser
poupado. Em verdade, não falamos nada; o muro falou por nós.
Não nos movemos, as mãos é que se estenderam pouco a pouco,
todas quatro, pegando-se, apertando-se, fundindo-se.

I turned toward her; Capitu had her eyes on the ground. She
raised them, slowly, and we stood staring at each other... Confession of children, thou art easily worth two or three pages, but I
must hurry along. The truth is, we said nothing: the wall spoke
for us. We did not move. It was our hands that stretched out, little
by little, all four of them, catching hold of each other, tightening
their grasp, melting one into the other. (chap. 14)

The atmosphere has suddenly shifted from one of repressed
communication to one of pure nonverbal confession in which
sparks of energy seem to sizzle the air as they jump back and
forth between the two adolescents. Another small rebirth
pattern has been depicted.

It would be impractical to try to mention here every instance
of the progression-regression pattern, for when we consider how
often the novel mentions the inability to speak, to walk, to
decide, to remember, or to act, in accompaniment with the
opposite effect at a later point, we realize that there are scores
of such occurrences.[12] As Bento himself points out, the shift
from depression to expansion, from introversion to extroversion
is his essence:

Já me sucedeu, aqui no Engenho Novo, por estar uma noite com
muita dor de cabeça, desejar que o trem da Central estourasse
longe dos meus ouvidos e interrompesse a linha por muitas horas,
ainda que morresse alguém; e no dia seguinte, perdi o trem da
mesma estrada, por ter ido dar a minha bengala a um cego que
não trazia bordão. *Voilà mes gestes, voilà mon essence.*

It recently happened here in Engenho Novo that one night when
I had a bad headache I wished one of the trains of the Central
would be blown up, far from my hearing, and the line interrupted
for many hours, even though someone should die; and on the
following day I missed a train of the same road because I stopped
to give my cane to a blind man who had no staff. *Voilà mes gestes,
voilà mon essence.* (chap. 68)

An examination of the cycle in one more sequence—the
crucial scenes in which Bentinho contemplates murder or
suicide and later accuses Capitu—will suffice to show the
importance of this "microscopic" pattern in the novel. Let us
begin by viewing Bentinho's ruminations after witnessing a
production of *Othello*:

—E [Desdêmona] era inocente, vinha eu dizendo rua abaixo;

—Que faria o público, se ela deveras fosse culpada, tão culpada como Capitu? E que morte lhe daria o mouro? Um travesseiro não bastaria; era preciso sangue, e fogo, um fogo intenso e vasto, que a consumisse de todo, e a reduzisse a pó, e o pó seria lançado ao vento, como eterna extinção.

"And [Desdemona] was innocent!" I kept saying to myself all the way down the street. "What would the audience do if she were really guilty, as guilty as Capitu? And what death would the Moor mete out to her then? A bolster would not suffice; there would be need of blood and fire, a vast, intense fire to consume her wholly, and reduce her to dust, and the dust tossed to the wind, in eternal extinction. (chap. 135)

Bentinho leaves the theater with the conviction that Capitu must die. Soon, however, the energy of that conviction as with so many others, subsides into nothingness. Bentinho says, "Vaguei pelas ruas o resto da noite" (I roamed through the streets the rest of the night—chap. 135). The verb "vagar" shows confusion, fluctuation, and lack of resolve. But then his powers for action seem to resurge, this time in the form of a different resolution:

Vi as últimas horas da noite e as primeiras do dia, vi os derradeiros passeadores e os primeiros varredores, as primeiras carroças, os primeiros ruídos, os primeiros albores, um dia que vinha depois do outro e me veria ir para nunca mais voltar. . . . A gente que passava não era tanta, como nos dias comuns da semana, mas era já numerosa e ia a algum trabalho, que repetiria depois; eu é que não repetiria mais nada.

I saw the last hours of night and the first hours of day. I saw the late strollers and the first sweepers, the first carts, the first noises, the first white streaks of day, a day that came after the other and would see me depart never to return. . . . There were not so many people on the street as on weekdays but there were quite a number off to tasks they would do again; but I would never do anything again. (chap. 135)

Bentinho seems at this moment to feel the rhythmic succession of life as an endless process of days and nights, rising and falling aspirations. He wants no further part of the continual repetition and decides that he, and not Capitu, should die. He buys poison. Later, while waiting for a servant to bring the coffee in which he will dissolve the venom, he lays hold of a volume of Plutarch, as if to infuse himself in the manner of

Cato with the energy to carry out the act: "Tinha necessidade de incutir em mim a coragem dele," he says, "assim como ele precisara dos sentimentos do filósofo, para intrepidamente morrer" (I had to arouse in myself the same courage, just as he had required the thoughts of the philosopher to die intrepidly —chap. 136). Evidently there has been another decline in his resolve, requiring such an infusion of courage.

When he is about to drink the poison, Ezequiel runs into the room:

> —Papai! papai!
>
> Leitor, houve aqui um gesto que eu não descrevo por havê-lo inteiramente esquecido, mas crê que foi belo e trágico. Efetiva-mente, a figura do pequeno fez-me recuar até cair de costas na estante.

> "Papa! Papa!"
>
> Reader, at this point there was a gesture that I will not describe because I have completely forgotten it, but believe me, it was beautiful and tragic. Practically speaking, the appearance of the little boy made me retreat until I knocked against the bookcase. (chap. 136)

The verb "recuar" suggests the shrinking, retreating motion of a dying impulse. But in a moment, Bentinho feels a renewed impetus: ". . . o meu primeiro ímpeto foi correr ao café e bebê-lo. Cheguei a pegar na xícara, mas o pequeno beijava-me a mão, como de costume, e a vista dele, como o gesto, deu-me outro impulso" (. . . my first impulse was to run to the coffee and drink it. I went so far as to lift the cup, but the little boy was kissing my hand, as he always did, and the sight of him, as well as the gesture, gave me another impulse—chap. 137). Within a mere instant, then, there is the birth of one impulse, its death, and the birth of a second. The latter, of course, is to give the poisoned coffee to Ezequiel: "Ezequiel abriu a boca. Cheguei-lhe a xícara, tão trêmulo que quase a entornei. . . . Mas não sei que senti que me fez recuar. Pus a xícara em cima da mesa, e dei por mim a beijar doidamente a cabeça do menino" (Ezequiel opened his mouth. I brought the cup to his lips with such trembling that I almost spilt it, but ready to pour it down his throat in case the taste or the temperature was repugnant to him—for the coffee was cold.... But I felt some-thing, I do not know what, that made me draw back. I set the cup on the table, and found myself wildly kissing the child's head—chap. 137). The second impulse also dies before it is carried out. Then a third arises and succeeds in reaching the point of action: ". . . dei por mim a beijar doidamente a cabeça do menino."

In the ensuing confrontation between Bentinho and Capitu, there are various other instances where Bentinho's emotional state shifts from being "a pique de crer que era vítima de uma grande ilusão" (on the brink of believing myself victim of a grand illusion—chap. 139) to being restored to a strong conviction of his wife's guilt. By the time Capitu and Ezequiel have returned from mass, "um homem novo" (a new man—chap. 140) seems to have been born within Bentinho, supplying the force necessary to replace his previous ambivalence with solid conviction:

> —Confiei a Deus todas as minhas amarguras, disse-me Capitu ao voltar da igreja; ouvi dentro de mim que a nossa separação, é indispensável, e estou às suas ordens.
>
> Os olhos com que me disse isto eram embuçados, como espreitando um gesto de recusa ou de espera. Contava com a minha debilidade ou com a própria incerteza em que eu podia estar da paternidade do outro, mas falhou tudo. Acaso haveria em mim um homem novo, um que aparecia agora, desde que impressões novas e fortes o descobriam: Nesse caso era um homem apenas encoberto. Respondi-lhe que ia pensar, e faríamos o que eu pensasse. Em verdade vos digo que tudo estava pensado e feito.
>
> "I confided all my bitterness to God," Capitu said to me on her return from church. "I heard within me the answer that our separation is inevitable, and I am at your disposal."
>
> Her eyes, as she said this, were masked, as though watching for a gesture of refusal or of delay. She was counting on my weakness or on my uncertainty concerning the paternity of the boy, but it was all to no avail. Could it be that there was a new man within me, the creation of new and strong pressures? If so, it was a man scarcely hidden beneath the surface. I replied that I would think it over, and we would do as I decided. To tell you the truth, it had all been thought over and decided. (chap. 140)

This last renaissance of Bentinho into "um homem novo" is dark and ironic, for instead of being a rebirth in the direction of optimism or viability, it points toward skepticism, misanthropy, and intransigence. Bentinho earlier could not muster the resolution necessary to kill himself. Now, as "um homem novo" he acquires the determination required to effect a permanent separation from his wife. Ironically, this separation amounts to a sort of spiritual suicide.

Ironic Rebirth

The emergence of this new man, Dom Casmurro, is one important case of ironic rebirth at the novel's end. However, the irony goes even further. In chapter 1, commenting on the structure of the novel and its correspondence with the quest myth, I mentioned that the cycle of the quest is completed when Bentinho and Capitu are married and that the remainder of the novel's plot constitutes an ironic inversion of the quest myth, ending not in triumphal return and reintegration, but in tragic separation. So far in this chapter, I have shown that the so-called rebirth pattern corresponds with the rising and falling fortunes of this mythic structure. Since the novel ends with a structural irony, it is interesting to note that there is an ironic rebirth accompanying that ending. This concerns the "resurrection" of Escobar in the person of Ezequiel.

To Bentinho, the most convincing piece of evidence for Capitu's unfaithfulness is the child Ezequiel's resemblance in gesture and appearance to Escobar. Eventually Bentinho can no longer stand even to be in the presence of the child because each time he looks upon him he can only see the resurrection of the man he believes betrayed him: "Escobar vinha assim surgindo da sepultura, do seminário e do Flamengo para se sentar comigo à mesa, receber-me na escada, beijar-me no gabinete da manhã, ou pedir-me à noite a bênção do costume. Todas essas ações eram repulsivas" (Escobar emerged from the grave, from the seminary, from Flamengo; he sat at table with me, welcomed me on the stairs, kissed me each morning in my study or asked for the customary blessing at night. All this repelled me—chap. 132). This "resurrection" is an indispensable factor in Bentinho's ultimate condemnation of Capitu. It is involved in what he considers the capstone of proof against her—an involuntary gesture, after he has accused her, of looking at Escobar's photograph when Ezequiel runs into the room:

> Palavra que estive a pique de crer que era vítima de uma grande ilusão, uma fantasmagoria de alucinado; mas a entrada repentina de Ezequiel, gritando: —"Mamãe! mamãe! é hora da missa!" restituiu-me à consciência da realidade. Capitu e eu, involuntariamente, olhamos para a fotografia de Escobar, depois um para o outro. Desta vez a confusão dela fez-se confissão pura. Este era aquele; havia por força alguma fotografia de Escobar pequeno que seria o nosso pequeno Ezequiel.

> Truthfully, I was on the brink of believing myself victim of a grand illusion, a madman's phantasmagoria; but the sudden

entrance of Ezequiel shouting, "Mamma! Mamma! it's time for
Mass" restored me to a sense of reality. Capitu and I, involuntarily, glanced at the photograph of Escobar, and then at each
other. This time her confusion was pure confession. They were
one; there must have been some photograph of Escobar as a little
boy which would be our little Ezequiel. (chap. 139)

Years later, when Ezequiel comes to visit, Bento will still see
him as a resurrection of Escobar:

> Estendeu o copo ao vinho que eu lhe oferecia, bebeu um gole, e
> continuou a comer. Escobar comia assim também, com a cara
> metida no prato. Contou-me a vida na Europa, os estudos,
> particularmente os de arqueologia, contava o Egito e os seus
> milhares de séculos, sem se parder nos algarismos; tinha a cabeça
> aritmética do pai. Eu, posto que a idéia da paternidade do outro
> me estivesse já familiar, não gostava da ressurreição. Às vezes,
> fechava os olhos para não ver gestos nem nada, mas o diabrete
> falava e ria, e o defunto falava e ria por ele.

> He held out his glass for the wine that I offered him, took a sip
> and went on eating. Escobar used to eat that way too, with his
> face in his plate. He told me about his life in Europe, his studies,
> particularly those in archaeology, which was his love. He spoke of
> antiquity with passion, ran through the story of Egypt with its
> thousands of ages without getting lost in the figures; he had his
> father's head for mathematics. Although the idea of the other's
> paternity was already familiar to me, I did not enjoy the
> resurrection. At times, I closed my eyes in order not to see
> gestures, or anything, but the rascal talked and laughed, and the
> dead man talked and laughed through him. (chap. 145)

Figure 3.3 is a modification of the original diagram of the
novel's plot structure, now taking into account the figurative
resurgence of Escobar in Ezequiel:

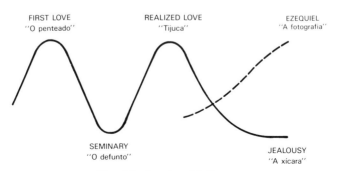

FIRST LOVE
"O penteado"

REALIZED LOVE
"Tijuca"

EZEQUIEL
"A fotografia"

SEMINARY
"O defunto"

JEALOUSY
"A xícara"

Fig. 3.3: Ironic rebirth

The divergence of the broken line, representing a vital surge, and the solid line, suggesting a decline in vitality, illustrates graphically irony's tension of opposing meanings. The final episodes of the novel depict a state of affective death in the protagonist. His attitude of cosmic suspicion is made heavier by the ironic presence of the youthful Ezequiel. In the end, even Ezequiel joins Capitu, D. Glória, Escobar, José Dias, and the others among the ranks of the dead.

Considering these characters, the status of life and death itself becomes ironic. Those characters who have been hopeful and active have gone to "estudar a geologia dos campos santos" (study the geology of holy ground—chap. 2), while the one character who has led the most stagnant and inactive existence is the ultimate survivor.

Matriarchy and Patriarchy

Machado de Assis consistently maintained that novels should have their basis in human nature rather than in circumstances or actions. In the preface to his first novel, for example, he stated that his aim was to delineate not manners, but two contrasting personalities: "Não quis fazer romance de costumes; tentei o esboço de uma situação e o contraste de dois caracteres" (I did not attempt to make a novel of manners; I sought after the outline of a situation and the contrast of two personalities).[1] This continued to be his goal, expressed in the preface to his second novel as well: "Convém dizer que o desenho de . . . caracteres . . . foi o meu objeto principal, senão exclusivo, servindo-me a ação apenas de tela em que lancei os contornos dos perfis" (Let it be said that the drawing of . . . personalities . . . was my principal, or even exclusive object, the action serving me merely as a canvas upon which I cast the contours of the profiles).[2]

Machado believed reliance upon circumstances rather than character traits to be the chief defect of Eça de Queirós' well-known novel, *O primo Basílio*. Machado's critique of the Portuguese novel may be thought of as a kind of *ars poetica*, setting forth his own standards as a novelist. He describes *O primo Basílio*'s adulterous protagonist, Luísa, as "matéria inerte" (inert matter),[3] "antes um títere do que uma pessoa moral" (more a puppet than a moral person)[4] and elaborates:

> Para que Luísa me atraia e me prenda, é preciso que as tribulações que a afligem venham dela mesma; seja uma rebelde ou uma arrependida; tenha remorsos ou imprecações; mas, por Deus! dê-me uma pessoa moral. Gastar o aço da paciência a fazer tapar a boca de uma cobiça subalterna, a substitui-la nos misteres ínfimos, a defendê-la dos ralhos do marido, é cortar todo o vínculo moral entre ela e nós. Já nenhuma há, quando Luísa adoece e morre. Por que? porque sabemos que a catástrofe é o resultado de uma circunstância fortuita, e nada mais. . . .

> In order for Luisa to attract and captivate me, the tribulations that afflict her must come from Luisa herself; let her be a rebel or a penitent; let her have remorse or imprecations; but for God's sake! give me a moral person. Wearing out one's patience by hushing up a subordinate's covetousness, doing her dirty chores for her, defending her from the husband's railings—it cuts off any moral attachment between her and us. There is no more left, when Luisa sickens and dies. Why? Because we know that the catastrophe is the result of a fortuitous circumstance, and nothing more. . . .[5]

When Machado says, "dê–me uma pessoa moral," we should understand that he is not referring to conventional morality. Luísa fails to be a "pessoa moral" not because she commits adultery, but rather because she displays few values, positive or negative—because her actions are not firmly rooted within her own nature. Machado criticized the lack of analysis of human nature in Luísa's characterization and found the novel in general likewise lacking. *O primo Basílio*'s unhappy ending involves love letters stolen by Luísa's housekeeper for blackmail. Machado calls the letters a fortuitous circumstance, and says that if the novel has a truth to convey, it can only be that "a boa escolha dos fâmulos é uma condição de paz no adultério" (the wise choice of servants is a condition for peace in adultery).[6]

Twelve years after writing his incisive critique of Eça's novel, Machado de Assis published *Dom Casmurro*. Machado's novel may be seen as his final answer to Eça de Queirós, for it treats the theme of adultery, the same we find in *O primo Basílio,* in terms of human nature instead of circumstance.

There are, to be sure, circumstances that play a major role in the unfolding of the novel: the fortunate arrangement of a substitute for Bentinho in the priesthood, Ezequiel's penchant for imitating others, and Escobar's drowning. But these do not determine the outcome of the story nearly so much as do the deeply rooted personalities of Capitu and Bentinho. In his earlier critique, Machado saw the difference between fortuitous, controlling circumstances and those that merely assist in bringing out the characters' passions. He cited the example of *Othello* to illustrate: "O lenço de Desdêmona tem larga parte na sua morte; mas a alma ciosa e ardente de Otelo, a perfídia de Iago e a inocência de Desdêmona, eis os elementos principais da ação" (Desdemona's handkerchief has a large part in her death; but the jealous and ardent soul of Othello, the treachery of Iago and the innocence of Desdemona—these are the principal elements of the action).[7]

The plan of outlining a situation and contrasting two personalities, by which Machado described his first novel, applies equally well to *Dom Casmurro*. The novel is a study of contrasting natures, and it is the contrasting natures of its protagonists, within a given situation, that determine the novel's action.

Here we will present a model for analyzing these opposing natures, by suggesting that the work can be seen as the antithesis of two underlying value systems—matriarchy and patriarchy—embodied respectively in the personalities of Capitu and Bentinho. The main characters' "moralidade" can be seen as a derivation of these primitive systems. As the differences between Bentinho and his wife become irreconcilable and the two are driven apart, both husband and wife act in a manner consistent with the values of matriarchy and patriarchy. This is not to suggest that the conflict between "matriarchy" and "patriarchy" as coherent ideologies is a conscious one on their part. Rather, we are speaking of the unconscious, archetypal underpinnings of the novel's drama of jealousy.[8] An analysis of the characters' behavior in terms of this dichotomy of value systems should help to demonstrate the universal concerns underlying Machado's novel. Taking this perspective, we are able to justify claims that the work is more than an account of domestic troubles. We can show that it resounds much more deeply, since the foundations of human relations within the family and the entire society are at play. In this light, we find there is little that is inconsistent or unmotivated in the conduct of either Capitu or Bentinho. Both, according to Machado's definition, are "pessoas morais."

We should recognize that this method, by emphasizing archetypes, tends to deemphasize the individuality of the novel's characters. Surely "pessoas morais" would be conscious of an individual set of ethics. Our approach does not disallow individuality; it merely looks beneath it and suggests that individual characteristics are the outgrowth of a collective system. The fact that Capitu's motives can be traced to the primitive code of matriarchy does not exclude personal motivation. The fact that we find evidences of patriarchy in Bentinho does not contradict such obvious individual traits as jealousy, a tendency to fantasize, a sense of insecurity, and so forth. Showing that the characters' motives are rooted in archetypal value systems, rather than denying individual character, should support it by demonstrating that the personal values, instead of being created *ex nihilo*, rest on universal human tendencies.

The "Yin" and "Yang" of the Quest

From the writings of various scholars[9] we may put together the following summary of values attributed to the contrasting systems:

Patriarchy	Matriarchy
1. Society tends to be authoritarian, stratified, based on hierarchy, birthright.	1. Society tends to be egalitarian, based on brotherly kinship, mother-right.
2. Emphasis is put on obedience to man-made law.	2. Emphasis is put on loyalty to ties of blood, ties with the soil.
3. Loyalty tends to be one-sided and "vertical"; for example, wife-to-husband, child-to-parent.	3. Loyalty tends to be reciprocal, "horizontal"; for example, mother-to-child, child-to-mother, child-to-child.
4. Fidelity is emphasized.	4. Fertility is emphasized
5. Achievement, merit, rationality, and honor are highly valued.	5. Brotherhood, charity, human life, and emotions are highly valued.
6. Man is mobile; tries to change, dominate natural world.	6. Man is sedentary; accepts, harmonizes with natural world.

7. Thinking tends to be cate-gorical, absolute.	7. Thinking tends to be rela-tivistic.

These sets of values involve different ways of gaining and exercising power. Both originate within the family and probably arise from the different biological capacities of mother and father. Because the mother is physically equipped not only to give birth, but also to nurse her babies, she is endowed with a *natural* superiority of influence over her children (note that *natural* comes from the Latin *natus* or *nascor,* terms relating to birth). The children, after all, are indisputably hers. The fact that the father's procreative contribution is nine months removed from birth gives him a natural inferiority of influence over the children, since barring sophisticated testing he can never be positive that the children are his. The more this biological superiority of influence is exploited, the more a society tends toward matriarchy. Sexual relations may tend to be promiscuous, or women may be prone to discard their mates after the men have served their reproductive purpose. Taking a lesson from their own bodies' more or less spontaneous productive capacity, the matriarchs establish an economy based on agriculture or on gathering the spontaneous fruits of the earth rather than on hunting, herding, building, trading, or other such mobile or labor-intensive pursuits.

In its extreme form, matriarchy alienates the males. To compensate for this alienating tendency, a more or less artificial set of influences has been manufactured. By subduing the earth and taking advantage of their superior physical strength, men have gained power in artifice to counterbalance women's biological influence. The strength of man's conquering the natural world is in more and better food, more comfortable shelter—products attractive even to matriarchs. In order to have better provisions for themselves and their offspring, the tendency is for matriarchs to let their mates become a part of the family. Acceptance of men implies a father's right to influence over his offspring and the mother's sexual fidelity so that the father can know that his children are indeed his. Once these concessions are made, man-made law has a reason for being, and men have a fulcrum with which to pry away at the matriarchal influence. The artificial (*ars*—craft or trade, and *facio*—to build or erect) exists in opposition to the natural in the power-play of human relations. In extreme forms of patriarchy, women are oppressed, and mother-right gives way almost entirely to the principle of authority and directive. The stratified, law-bound, dutiful orientation of patriarchy takes over.

These two opposing tendencies are part of the central myth underlying the novel. As I brought out in chapter 3, the quest myth and the rebirth pattern are analogous in structure and function. Chapters 1, 2, and 3 demonstrate that in the case of *Dom Casmurro,* the two are intertwined and inseparable. The same may be said for numerous other so-called rebirth stories or quests. They are, in effect, different orientations of the same underlying myth.[10] The quest myth tends to have a patriarchal orientation because it emphasizes mobility, domination over external forces through physical prowess, achievement, and often nobility or birthright. The rebirth pattern tends toward a matriarchal orientation because it stresses natural cycles, spontaneous fruition, and preservation of life.

Actually, both sides of the myth are often contained in what are normally called quests. When the hero exhausts his physical powers against his formidable enemy, appears to have been defeated, and is then miraculously restored through no effort of his own, we are witnessing the emergence of the matriarchal component of the myth. Quests, therefore, often have both a "Yin" and a "Yang." In *Dom Casmurro,* where the "hero" is not endowed with the normal physical gifts, the "Yin" is indeed a prominent aspect.

Perhaps pure matriarchy and pure patriarchy are impossible extremes, never really verifiable in the history of the race. Though they may gravitate toward one pole or the other, societies are characterized by the fusion and tension of both systems. In any case, we are not interested so much in the historical validity of either system as we are in the theoretical applicability of both as a duality of opposing values.

Antithesis and Synthesis in the Novel

In *Dom Casmurro,* Bentinho and Capitu both exhibit attitudes, dispositions, and actions consistent with the ideologies discussed. At first they both show a healthy combination of the two. Bentinho has a clumsy passivity but in submitting to Capitu's flirtation begins to take a more active role and to discover his manly identity. Capitu is manipulative and dominant but also spontaneous and at times submissive. But as the novel unfolds, Bentinho becomes so identified with patriarchal values, and Capitu with those of matriarchy, as to become incarnations of the value systems themselves.

The relationship of the characters and their positions is most clearly seen in the novel during moments of antagonism. One good textual example appears in what Bento calls a "duelo de ironias" (duel of ironies) between him and Capitu. Bentinho and Capitu are faced with the challenge of circumventing D. Glória's promise to give Bentinho to the priesthood. When Capitu ironically suggests that Bentinho go ahead and become a priest, the following dialog ensues:

—Pois, sim, Capitu, você ouvirá a minha missa nova, mas com uma condição.
Ao que ela respondeu:
—Vossa Reverendíssima pode falar.
—Promete uma cousa?
—Que é?
—Diga se promete.
—Não sabendo o que é, não prometo.
A falar a verdade são duas coisas, continuei eu, por haver-me acudido outra idéia.
—Duas? Diga quais são.
—A primeira é que só te hás de confessar comigo, para eu lhe dar a penitência e a absolvição. A segunda é que...
—A primeira está prometida, disse ela vendo-me hesitar, e acrescentou que esperava a segunda.
Palavra que me custou, e antes não me chegasse a sair da boca; não ouviria o que ouvi, e não escreveria aqui uma coisa que vai talvez achar incrédulos.
—A segunda... sim... é que... Promete-me que seja eu o padre que case você?
—Que me case? disse ela um tanto comovida.
Logo depois fez descair os lábios, e abanou a cabeça.
—Não, Bentinho, disse, seria esperar muito tempo; você não vai ser padre já amanhã, leva muitos anos... Olhe, prometo outra coisa; prometo que há de batizar o meu primeiro filho.

"Of course, Capitu, you shall hear my first Mass, but upon one condition.
She answered, "Your Reverence may speak."
"Will you promise one thing?"
"What is it?"
"Say whether you promise."
"I won't promise without knowing what it is."
"To tell the truth there are two things," I went on, for another idea had come to me.
"Two? Tell me what they are."

"The first is that you confess only to me, I alone shall give you penance and absolution. The second is ..."

"The first is promised," said Capitu as she saw me hesitate, and she added that she was waiting to hear the second.

What it cost me to get it out, and would that it had never passed my lips! I would not have heard what I heard, and I would not have to write here something that one may find hard to believe.

"The second ... yes ... is this.... Promise me that I shall be the padre who marries you."

"Who marries me?" she echoed a little shaken.

Then she drooped the corners of her mouth and shook her head. "No, Bentinho," she said. "It would mean waiting a long time. You are not going to become a padre over night. It takes many years ... Look, I'll promise something else: I promise that you shall baptize my first child." (chap. 44)

The polarity between the characters at this point can be summarized with the following diagram:

Patriarchy		Matriarchy
Bentinho	X	Capitu
(Priest)		(Mother)

The words in parentheses represent what each character would presumably become if he or she were to be completely guided by the patriarchal or matriarchal system of values. Bentinho would become a priest within a patriarchal church. The name "padre," and Capitu's sarcastic address of respect, "Vossa Reverendíssima," suggest the patriarchal and authoritative quality of the priestly office. By having Capitu promise that she would confess to him, Bentinho shows that his position would entitle him to expect an accounting for the actions of others and to enable him to pass judgment on the righteousness of the actions according to ecclesiastic law. By having Capitu promise that she would let him perform her marriage ceremony, he reveals that he would expect to be able to sanction her actions and the actions of others and that such sanction would be called for. He also reveals that by assuming that position of authority, he would necessarily repudiate the possibility of being married. On the other hand, by promising to let Bentinho baptize her first child, Capitu focuses upon a central value of the matriarchal system—creating offspring. She also makes it painfully clear that in order to fulfill that goal, she would be willing to repudiate her relationship with

Bentinho and find another man to father the child. We note that Bentinho is more concerned with marital fidelity than with fertility since his promise has to do with the marriage ceremony, not the baptism. Capitu's promise shows an opposing emphasis. In the conversation she de-emphasizes the marriage, in keeping with the matriarchal bias, and emphasizes the fruit of the marriage.[11]

Since the attitude demonstrated in the dialog is antagonistic, the polarity of the two positions is easily seen. However, during much of the novel, the attitudes and efforts of these characters are conciliatory, as they attempt to establish a synthesis of the two contrasting natures. That possibility for reconciliation offers itself in the form of a trusting, fruitful marriage.

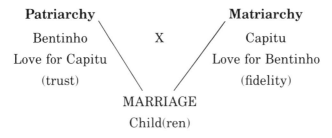

Patriarchy   **Matriarchy**

Bentinho   X   Capitu

Love for Capitu   Love for Bentinho

(trust)   (fidelity)

MARRIAGE

Child(ren)

The force that precipitates this movement toward compromise is a mutual attraction, which prompts each person to make concessions. The concessions are shown in the above diagram. Bentinho's compromise calls for dispensing with the patriarchal requirement for absolute accountability on the part of his partner. Since it is not practical or fashionable in modern society for a man to make his wife a prisoner, a husband cannot be absolutely certain that his children are really his. He must therefore trust his wife and be willing to accept whatever signs of fidelity she may be willing to give without demanding proof. On the part of Capitu, the necessary compromise is to be faithful to a single mate and perhaps to submit to an accounting for her behavior. If this synthesis were to function properly, the natural result would be a reasonably harmonious family with one or more children, through which the father satisfies his need to have a society to direct and organize, and the mother satisfies her need to create and influence offspring. It seems that marriages, as well as the societies for which marriage tends to be a microcosm, thrive on the compromise of patriarchy and matriarchy. The absence of this compromise leads to laxness and stagnation on the one extreme, and subjugation and alienation on the other. The co-existence of these systems depends upon mutual concessions. It is evident that in *Dom Casmurro* such a harmonizing synthesis is not the final outcome. The remainer of this chapter will examine how Bentinho and Capitu take steps, in spite of their mutual love, that affirm their monolithic positions as representatives of the disparate orders.

Bentinho as Patriarch

Bentinho's appreciation for patriarchal values is often coupled with an excessive concern about his masculinity. In society these elements do not have to be connected, but they perhaps tend to be. In the novel they clearly are. For example, consider Bentinho's jealousy of a horseback-riding dandy in his neighborhood. Besides the obvious explanation that Bentinho thinks the dandy is flirting with Capitu, there are a couple of underlying explanations for his jealousy. One is a connection, perhaps subconscious, between horseback riding and manliness. In this regard, we recall Bentinho's description of his first unsuccessful experience on horseback and his explanation that he later learned to ride, more out of shame for his inability than out of desire to ride. His explanation that people commented as he began to learn, "Agora é que ele vai namorar deveras" (Now he is really going to take an interest in the girls—chap. 6), shows a mental connection between horseback riding and virility. But another more deep-seated explanation has to do with patriarchal values: the horse is a symbol of mobility; therefore, being able to control a horse suggests adherence to patriarchy's ethic of dominance and mobility. This esteem for mobility finds further corroboration in Bentinho's fascination with coaches, as seen in the chapter entitled "A sege" (The chaise). The case of horses and horseback riders suggests the various psychological strata that can be analyzed in the characters' actions. Here we see motives on the level of conventional role expectations: Bentinho is jealous because boyfriends are supposed to act jealous in his society. At the same time, we detect a deeper plane of motivation having to do with his insecurity as a man. Yet there is a still more profound stratum, based upon universal tensions between matriarchy and patriarchy, which subsumes the others and places them in a broader context. Interpretations of the characters' actions in terms of societal conventions or of unconscious psychological needs are therefore not in opposition to an interpretation considering matriarchy and patriarchy. Instead, this deeply rooted structure may be seen as a foundation for the others, which are to some degree epiphenomena.

In his relationship with Capitu, Bentinho displays the tendency to give directions and be possessive. When José Dias incites Bentinho's jealousy by mentioning the possibility that some "peralta da vizinhança" (young buck of the neighborhood) may sweep Capitu away and marry her, Bentinho shows his propensity to regard Capitu as a possession: "Agora lembrava-me que alguns [peraltas] olhavam para Capitu, —e tão senhor me sentia dela que era como se olhassem para mim, um simples dever de admiração e de inveja" (Now I remembered that some [dandies] used to stare at Capitu—and I had felt myself so lord of her that it was as if they had stared at me, a simple tribute of admiration and envy—chap. 62). Bentinho's confessions about his longing to have a son reveal the patriarchal, possessive character of his values, for he describes his "sede de um filho, . . . um filho próprio da minha pessoa" (longing for a child, . . . a child of my own body—chap. 108). This attitude, a common and conventional one in modern society, has its foundations in patriarchy's emphasis on artificial law. Personal possessions tend to be absent in matriarchy's communal orientation. Patriarchy's man-made law in effect creates the concept of personal property and encourages the inclusion of human beings within the concept. Bentinho, being both a lawyer and a jealous husband, symbolizes the compatibility of possessiveness and a bias in favor of man-made law.

In spite of his lack of personal charisma, Bentinho desires to play the role of the dominating, directing patriarch. The account of Capitu and Bentinho's marriage ceremony shows how Bentinho gives importance to suggestions that the wife should be submissive in marriage. He remembers the scriptural citation from Peter, read at the wedding: "As mulheres sejam sujeitas a seus maridos... Do mesmo modo, vós, maridos, coabitai com elas, tratando-as com honra, como a vasos mais fracos, . . ." (Ye wives, be in subjection to your husbands. . . . Likewise, ye husbands, dwell with them, giving honor unto the wife as unto the weaker vessel—chap. 101). Capitu does not grasp these words at the time because they are in Latin, but Bentinho makes sure she knows about them, for he explains to her later what was said. That he intends to make his wife submissive, and that she is willing to cooperate to an extent, is shown in the chapter in which Bentinho commands Capitu to quit showing her bare arms in public. In the same chapter he reveals that he has prevailed on her to quit singing because of her poor singing voice (chap. 105).

Bentinho perceives the relationship hierarchically. Since he is of a higher social standing and more educated, Bentinho feels he has a right to instruct Capitu on various matters. The episode in which he becomes jealous of the sea (the sea steals her attention away from him during an astronomy lesson) is a good example. The same chapter refers to the economic hierarchy in the family, in which Bentinho gives Capitu an allowance (chap. 106). Bentinho's authoritative disposition is at least partially a product of his home life; even though he has not had the benefit of a father to raise him, he has definite ideas about his father's place in the family. His mother remains extremely loyal to her husband, even long after his death. She wears mourning clothes for the rest of her life and refuses to move from the house on Rua Matacavalos, where they lived their last two years together. On his wall, Bento keeps a portrait of his mother and father. His description of the picture shows how he perceives the father's role to be authoritarian and possessive: "São retratos que valem por originais. O de minha mãe, estendendo a flor ao marido, parece dizer: 'Sou toda sua, meu guapo cavalheiro!' O de meu pai, olhando para a gente, faz este comentário: 'Vejam como esta moça me quer...' " (They are portraits that could pass for originals. The one of my mother, holding the flower toward her husband, seems to say: "I am all yours, my gallant cavalier!" That of my father, looking out at us, makes this commentary, "See how the girl loves me..."—chap. 7). That his father was the controlling force in the household is suggested when Bento admits that if his father had lived, D. Glória probably would have been dissuaded from her promise to make him a priest, and he would have followed his father into a political career (chap. 130).

Capitu as Matriarch

Capitu, on the other hand, seems to have been brought up in a predominantly matriarchal household. It is her mother, D. Fortunata, at times relying on the influence of D. Glória, who seems to direct matters in the family. This dominance is displayed on at least two occasions: when the two women convince

Pádua to spend his lottery prize money to buy a house rather than more extravagant things, and when they dissuade him from killing himself when his interim administration comes to an end (chap. 16). Here Pádua's concern for honor and social position gives way to the matriarchal emphasis on sustaining human life.

Whereas Bentinho tends to rely on traditional authority figures for help in escaping the seminary, Capitu takes a different course. Bentinho imagines appealing to D. Pedro II to achieve absolution from D. Glória's promise. Capitu's advice to Bentinho, to leave the Emperor in peace and count on José Dias' intervention with D. Glória, shows that she perceives decision-making power to rest with the mother and to be more subject to internal influences than external, hierarchical pressures (chap. 31). At the same time, Capitu seems to recognize the strong motivation behind the authoritarian principles of honor and control and to be able to encourage those values when they can be put to work for her purposes. Capitu displays this ability when she seeks to bring out Bentinho's desire to go against his mother by appealing to his sense of manliness with the question: "Você tem medo?" (Are you afraid—chap. 43).

Capitu's association with matriarchy is not so obvious as Bentinho's with patriarchy, probably because her description is marked by Bentinho's patriarchal bias. For example, Bentinho seems to accuse Capitu of being a social climber, giving such examples as her "curiosidades" (curiosities), which he implies show her desire to ingratiate herself with members of the Santiago household (chap. 31), and her desire for an early end to their honeymoon in Tijuca, which he says was motivated by her need to show off her new husband before the world (chap. 102). However, if we admit that his evaluations are tempered with the perspective of one who thinks in hierarchical terms, we can see her actions as demonstrations of matriarchal values. Her eagerness to be with members of a higher class may simply show that class distinctions are unimportant to her and that she is interested in people and things in general. In addition, her desire to return home during the honeymoon may have really been prompted by concern for relatives, as she insisted it was.

Two significant incidents show how Capitu tends to value the matriarchal side of the antithesis. The first of these is the "juramento do poço" (Oath at the well). Under the threat of being sent to the seminary, Bentinho proposes an oath that would ensure mutual commitment. Capitu accepts Bentinho's oath, but then proposes a slightly amended oath of her own:

> Você jura uma coisa? Jura que só há de casar comigo?
> Capitu não hesitou em jurar, e até lhe vi as faces vermelhas de prazer. Jurou duas vezes e uma terceira:
> —Ainda que você case com outra, cumprirei o meu juramento, não casando nunca.
> —Que eu case com outra?
> —Tudo pode ser, Bento. Você pode achar outra moça que lhe queira, apaixonar-se por ela e casar. Quem sou eu para você lembrar-se de mim nessa ocasião?
> —Mas eu também juro! Juro, Capitu, juro por Deus Nosso Senhor que só me casarei com você. Basta isto?
> —Devia bastar, disse ela; eu não me atrevo a pedir mais. Sim, você jura... Mas juremos por outro modo; juremos que nos havemos de casar um com outro, haja o que houver.

> "Will you swear to something? Will you swear to marry no one but me?"
> Capitu did not hesitate to swear, and I even saw her cheeks redden with pleasure. She swore twice and a third time.
> "Even if you marry someone else, I'll keep my oath and never marry—ever."
> "If I marry someone else?"
> "Anything can happen, Bentinho. You may find another girl that likes you, fall in love, and marry her. Who am I for you to remember me at such a time?"
> "But I too swear! I *swear,* Capitu, I swear by Almighty God that I will marry no one but you. Is that enough?"
> "It should be," she replied. "I dare not ask more. Yes, you have sworn ... But let us swear in another manner. Let us swear that we will marry each other, come what may." (chap. 48)

Capitu's acceptance of the first oath seems to be offered as a catalyst for the second oath. Ever so subtly ("Eu não me atrevo a pedir mais") she succeeds in affecting a covenant that suits her purposes more closely. Bentinho's oath—"que só há de casar comigo"—emphasizes exclusiveness, but not necessarily obligation to marry. In keeping with the patriarchal ethos, the value of fidelity is supreme. But Capitu's oath—"que nos havemos de casar um com outro, haja o que houver"—leaves no possibility for mutual celibacy. Hers, in accordance with the matriarchal value system, emphasizes the potential for fertility.

A second incident suggesting their respective orientations is that in which Capitu expresses distaste at José Dias' use of the phrase "filho do homem" (son of man):

> Desta vez falou ao modo bíblico (estivera na véspera a folhear o livro de Ezequiel, como soube depois) e perguntava-lhe: "Como vai isso, filho do homem?" "Dize-me, filho do homem, onde estão os teus brinquedos?" "Queres comer doce, filho do homem?"
> —Que filho do homem é esse? perguntou Capitu agastada.
> —São os modos de dizer da Bíblia.
> —Pois eu não gosto deles, replicou ela com aspereza.
> —Tem razão, Capitu, concordou o agregado.

> This time he spoke in the Biblical manner (he had been leafing through the book of Ezekiel the night before as I later learned), and asked him, "How goes it, son of man?" "Tell me, son of man, where are your toys?" "Would you like a sweet, son of man?"
> "What's this son of man business?" asked Capitu sharply.
> "It's the manner of speaking of the Bible."
> "Well, I don't like it," she replied.
> "You are right, Capitu," agreed the dependent. (chap. 116)

No explicit explanation is offered for Capitu's irritation. The narrator implies that the phrase bothers Capitu because it calls attention to Ezequiel's illicit paternity. That may or may not be true.[12] There is also ample justification for her displeasure with the expression "filho do homem" within the context of a matriarchal predisposition. "Filho do homem" is full of patriarchal associations because it emphasizes ties to the father and excludes the mother. Capitu perhaps detests the phrase instinctively for that very reason—as far as she is concerned, Ezequiel is really "filho da mulher" (son of woman). Whether or not Capitu has been unfaithful to her husband, anything that may call attention to the link of possession between father and son will be unpleasant for her if she identifies sufficiently with the values of a matriarch.

In terms of action, Capitu favors mother-right with her tendency to be unconventional, impulsive, and free from restraints. She is fluid rather than rigid in her behavior. Her physical description harmonizes with this fluidity and further strengthens her association with matriarchy. Certainly her "olhos de ressaca" (undertow eyes) are her most striking physical attribute. The image of the "ressaca," in the sense of "tide," suggests the lunar cycle, natural time as opposed to artificial time, ebb and flow, and other concepts traditionally associated with matriarchal consciousness.[13]

The Failure of Reconciliation

The obstacles to the desired reconciliation between Capitu and Bentinho are embodied in two important characters—D. Glória and Escobar. D. Glória's promise to make her son a priest, if she should be granted one, is the first threat against compromise. Making promises, an exercise of artificial influence *par excellence,* is a significant propensity of both D. Glória and her son.

If D. Glória had not been eventually satisfied that she had fulfilled her promise by sponsoring a substitute, Bentinho might have become a Catholic priest. The priesthood is surely a position of authority in a patriarchal order. The office's celibacy is important within the novel, for in its detachment from marriage it suggests the irreconcilability of extreme patriarchy with matriarchy, or even with a compromised version thereof. Thus, although D. Glória is a mother and may behave in a typically "feminine" way, she should not be considered a proponent of matriarchy. Rather, she reinforces patriarchy and tends to influence Bentinho in that direction, not only by encouraging him to become a priest, but also, and more importantly, by teaching him those values through extreme loyalty to her deceased husband. Once Capitu and Bentinho overcome the threat of the seminary and priesthood, D. Glória becomes a relatively unimportant character in the novel. Her influence, however, stays with Bentinho until the end as he becomes increasingly insistent on his authoritarian values.

Escobar's threat to reconciliation is ambiguous. He either becomes Capitu's partner in adultery and fathers her child, or he does nothing more than display more friendship and intimacy for Capitu, and receive more in turn, than Bentinho is willing to accept. Either way, Escobar is a character who does not "play along" with patriarchal ethics and who pushes Capitu toward her exclusive position. His presence in the novel helps cause Capitu and Bentinho to affirm their uncompromising natures. Bentinho's jealousy, arising from his insecurity, is excited because Escobar has succeeded in fathering a child, while he has not, and because Escobar is stronger physically and more disposed to subdue natural forces.[14] When Escobar drowns, Bentinho encounters the confirming sign for his already-active suspicions when he sees Capitu over his friend's body. He assumes the worst. He perceives the display of sympathy in patriarchal terms as a display of "vertical" loyalty from wife to husband, when in all likelihood, whether she has been unfaithful or not, Capitu's sympathy is more "horizontal," showing bonds of affection like those between sister and a brother. From that point onward, Bentinho cannot look upon the boy Ezequiel without seeing Escobar arising from the grave.

Capitu recognizes her husband's suspicions and by refusing to try to give him assurance that Ezequiel is his son, takes a position decidedly unsympathetic to that of patriarchy. In the final confrontation between Bentinho and Capitu, we see patriarch and matriarch squared off against each other. He pronounces his accusation and makes it clear who he believes is the father. Assuming a position similar to that of a priest, the sovereign father he appears destined to become, he demands a confession from her.[15] But Capitu, as if to deny the validity of a system that requires fidelity to a single man, or even an accounting for one's sexual contacts, offers not a word in her own defense. The conciliatory forces—trust on the one side, and willingness to invite trust on the other—have been repudiated.

Bentinho separates himself from Capitu and her son. The distance of that separation—the parties remain on opposite sides of the Atlantic ocean—emphasizes the inability of the two value systems to be reconciled in this particular case. Ezequiel, who might otherwise have come to represent the harmonizing synthesis of the two values, loses his mother, loses his father (whether literally, through death, or otherwise), and dies, like an exiled orphan, of a strange disease in a strange land.

In this dramatic clash between opposites, Bentinho and Capitu champion their respective causes to the extent of excluding consideration of all others. A compromise between the antitheses is approached through Bentinho and Capitu's marriage but is lost in the end. If there is in each a final recognition of the other's validity, it must be found in the sense of loss with which the characters affirm their rightness. They pursue their diverging causes to the very end but know and feel the costs of their insistence.

The failure to achieve reconciliation transforms Bentinho into a cynical misanthrope, a "Dom Casmurro." In the epithet applied to Bentinho, "Dom" effectively suggests the irony of his situation. The word stems from *dominus*—owner, commander, lord.[16] It is sometimes used as a title for high-ranking clergy. Bentinho's efforts as a youth were directed toward avoiding the clergy, yet through his own insistence he has achieved an ironically applied cleric's title. Though he may not be celibate in a strict sense, he is in the sense that he has repudiated marriage. Furthermore, Bentinho succeeds in becoming a "Dom" because he insists upon asserting his right to possess and command. Yet in doing so, he loses Capitu—his world, his only true vocation, the substance of life he most wanted to possess.

A Metaliterary Reading

The duality of matriarchy and patriarchy is analogous to opposing theories concerning the relationship between readers, authors, and works.[17] On the one hand, a literary work may be regarded from an "authoritarian" point of view, which is a parallel of patriarchy. It assumes that the text and its meanings derive from the author, the one who builds and manipulates it (this brings us back to the Latin *facere,* the same root we noticed in "artifice"). "Patriarchal" readers perceive the production of a literary work as a craft, requiring strength, perseverance, skill, and intelligence—literally, as a "work." What meanings a work contains are there by the intention and skill of the author. Interpretive reading is therefore an attempt to surmise the author's grand design and the means with which he accomplished that design.

Over the past several years critical movements have arisen in an attempt to disprove this "authoritarian" orientation, to show the "intentional fallacy" involved, and to propose alternative theories of the text's status. These efforts have culminated in several related points of view which are similar to, or even arise from, a matriarchal predisposition. Rather than perceiving a work's author as a controlling father, "matriarchal" readers tend to perceive the author as a mother-figure, someone who is impregnated with literary traditions, social conventions, and an arbitrary set of linguistic "chromosomes," and who after an appropriate period of gestation realizes the fruits of her labor. The author, in essence, gives birth. The work is not so much a product of individual craft as a product of culture in all its dimensions. It consequently belongs more to society than to the author.

Dom Casmurro reveals the conflict between patriarchy and matriarchy which underlies many social and individual tensions. At the same time, the novel suggests the analogous conflict between opposing modes of reading. It does this by means of a complex metaphoric play involving textual authority, authorship, and paternity.

In the first chapter of the novel, Bento explains why the title of the work is not really his. "Dom Casmurro" was an appellation given to him by a young poetry reader traveling next to him through the city one day. Bento says:

> . . . não achei melhor título para a minha narração; se não tiver outro daqui até o fim do livro, vai este mesmo. O meu poeta do trem ficará sabendo que não lhe guardo rancor. E com pequeno esforço, sendo o título seu, poderá cuidar que a obra é sua. Há livros que apenas terão isso dos seus autores; alguns nem tanto.

> . . . I have found no better title for my narrative; if no better occurs, let it stand! My poet of the train will know that I do not bear him a grudge. And, with a little effort, since the title is his, he will be able to decide that the work is his. There are books which owe no more to their authors; some, not so much. (chap. 1)

The narrator here plays with the paradoxical idea that authors may not be authors of their own works. Some works, supposedly like the one Bento is writing, (1) have a title from another source but are otherwise completely the product of their authors. Other works (2) may have titles furnished by their authors but otherwise be attributable to someone else. Still, he says, there may be other works (3) with neither the titles nor the authorship of their supposed authors.

Here Bento seems to be obliquely referring to the paternity question which he will raise and attempt to substantiate throughout the course of the novel. The basis of the figurative language used here is an equivalence between authorship and paternity. Thus, Bento calls attention from the very beginning to the question of Ezequiel's "authorship," even before the child's mother has entered the scene. The narrator's contention is that cases two and three from the preceding paragraph apply to Ezequiel. The child is a book with one person's title and another's authorship in the sense that he bears the Santiago name but, as Bento believes, is the son of Escobar. In another sense, Ezequiel has neither the name nor the authorship of his putative author, since he is named after Escobar (chap. 108).

However, contrary to the intention of the narrator, the first case also seems applicable to Ezequiel. He may bear the name of another man but may nevertheless be the son of Bentinho. Just as the book Bento is writing has another man's title but is nevertheless Bento's book (we may disregard the notion on another level that it is actually Machado's), one interpretation of the novel is that Ezequiel, although he is called by another's name and even called another's son, is actually the son of the man married to his mother. The narrator clearly intends to show that he has been betrayed—that the child is not his—but despite the account's intention, by one interpretation it goes against itself and suggests the contrary. In this respect, and in direct opposition to Bento's metaphor equating authors and fathers, Bento's book is not really Bento's book at all. It says something he never intended it to say.

With its first-person pseudo-author and its ambiguous story involving the question of faithfulness, betrayal, and paternal attribution, *Dom Casmurro* has created for itself the ideal metaphorical territory for exploring the relationship between authors, works, and readers. The novel poses the question of whether an author's intention can be read or whether considerations of intention are relevant. Implied in this question is the problem of whether a work, once it is written, can ever really "belong" to its author. The theme of an author's pride in his creation, and his possessiveness of that creation, is an important one in the novel. But concomitantly, the theme of the reader's expropriation of another author's work is also important. The latter is perhaps the main point for the inclusion in the narrative of the *Panegírico de Santa Mônica*. A colleague of Bentinho's from the seminary has for years been distributing to friends copies of his pamphlet. Meeting Bentinho after several years, he asks, "Conservou o meu *Panegírico?*" (Did you keep my *Panegyric?*—chap. 54). Bentinho receives a copy and enjoys reading it immensely; however, the enjoyment comes not from the friend's intended panegyric so much as from the childhood memories it resuscitates in Bentinho as he reads it. The narrator is explicit about his expropriation of the book, saying he put into the *Panegyric* many things of his own (chap. 60). Bento generalizes: "É que tudo se acha fora de um livro falho, leitor amigo. Assim preencho as lacunas alheias; assim podes também preencher as minhas" (The fact is, everything is to be found outside a book that has gaps, gentle reader. This is the way I fill in other men's lacunae; in the same way you may fill in mine—chap. 59).

This process of circumventing the writer's supposed intentions, of filling in gaps and extracting one's own message, almost behind the author's back or over his dead body, is exactly what the reader of *Dom Casmurro* is apt to do with the narration offered by Santiago. Reading in this manner, we place ourselves in a position similar to that of a matriarch. We in essence deny the author's possessive right over the text and instead claim it as a possession of the community of readers, for each to use as he sees fit.

But matriarchal reading, like its patriarchal counterpart, has its pitfalls. While the latter outlook breeds rigidity and narrow-mindedness, the former breeds a kind of mental mushiness. If the reader is given complete liberty, then standards disappear. We become obliged to accept any reading as valid. But how many of us would go that far, accepting a reading, for example, in which José Dias is the father of Ezequiel?

It is not easy to take an entirely nonauthoritarian stance as a reader of *Dom Casmurro* without falling into similarly unfounded interpretations. We find "authority" in the novel for both sides of the dichotomy. The narrator gives us his evidence for supposing Capitu's guilt, but the same narrator (or perhaps the true author) gives us evidence supporting her innocence as well. If we go along with the narrator's accusation, we accept his intentions. If we accept the opposite interpretation, we go against his intentions, do we not? Not really, for even then we actually comply with his intentions, following his directions to "preencher as minhas [lacunas]." *Dom Casmurro* places the reader in a paradoxical situation. The novel in effect forces the reader to declare his liberty.

Machado's masterpiece presents in the characters Capitu and Bentinho a tension between matriarchy and patriarchy with a possibility for compromise in their marriage. Similarly, on a metaliterary level, the novel seems to call for a reconciliation through compromise—a marriage between an author-centered outlook and a reader-centered one, requiring each to make concessions to the other.

A Voyage through Undertow Eyes

Some sort of arduous voyage is implied in the basic formula of the quest myth, with its phases of separation, initiation, and return. Mobility can thus be considered one aspect of the power that is an essential characteristic of the archetypal hero. The greater the hero's ability to effect a separation from his original location, to surpass obstacles, to cross thresholds, and to return home again, the greater his heroism and his mythic quality.[1] Literally speaking, Bentinho is the opposite of a mythic hero. Instead of being physically dynamic, he is static. What traveling he does receives only the slightest attention in the novel. Bentinho apparently studies law in São Paulo, but there is hardly any mention of any travel involved, and the whole five-year university period is summarized in only two sentences (chap. 98). We know that he goes to Europe at least three times—once to leave Capitu in Switzerland, and twice to "enganar a opinião" (deceive opinion—chap. 141). These are brusque, dutiful trips, however, of little importance for Santiago and even less for the plot. They certainly have nothing to do with a quest.

But if in a literal sense Bentinho is an ever-stationary *carioca*, in a figurative sense he is a great traveler who deserves comparison with the heroes of the quest tradition. Through metaphor, Bentinho's trial-ridden voyage is transformed or displaced from the concrete pattern of the quest myth. Because of this transformation, the protagonist may lead a bourgeois existence in a realistic urban setting and at the same time retain vestiges of a hero in a supernatural world, fighting against absolute forces. The device of metaphor thus allows for the copresence of myth and modernity in the novel.

The Quest and the Metaphoric Sea Voyage

Given the possibilities of a voyage over land, in the water, or through air space, it is not surprising that Machado de Assis chose the water as his medium for Bentinho's figurative travels. As I will try to show later, the novel responds to a literary tradition, and within the Portuguese-speaking world, the sea voyage is a particularly potent and abiding theme.

Numerous figurative statements establish an equivalence between Bentinho's life and a sea journey. Discussing with the old tenor, Marcolini, the theory that life is an opera, Bento says that life could just as well be "uma viagem de mar ou uma batalha" (a voyage at sea or a battle—chap. 9). Describing his bargain with God to obtain a release from his mother's promise, the narrator says that what was at stake was "a salvação ou o naufrágio da minha existência inteira" (the salvation or the shipwreck of my entire existence—chap. 20). He refers to life's aspirations as "a ilha dos sonhos" (the isle of dreams—chap. 64), implying the necessity of a sea voyage to reach them. Comparing purgatory and hell, he calls the latter "o eterno naufrágio" (eternal shipwreck—chap. 114).

Santiago clearly uses many metaphors to refer to life, destiny, or the universe. Life is an opera, a war, a drama, a house, a religious ceremony, a lottery, and even a loan. Judging by sheer force of repetition, however, it would seem that the predominant metaphor for life is the sea voyage. Bento's life is consistently defined, metaphorically, in those mythical and heroic terms.

His interaction with Capitu is by no means a trivial part of that life. On the contrary, that relationship *is* his life. It is important to realize that the narrator repeatedly gives the interchange the metaphoric dimension of a maritime voyage. He narrates his memorable first kiss with Capitu in the terms of a sea exploration, admitting that "Colombo não teve maior

orgulho, descobrindo a América" (Columbus felt no greater
[pride] when he discovered America—chap. 34). He describes
the promise that he and Capitu made to marry as a secure port
in which they should have taken refuge much earlier. He
justifies their delay by saying "não se navegam corações como
os outros mares deste mundo" (hearts are not navigated like
the other seas of this world—chap. 49). He depicts periods of
marital trouble as maritime storms and describes moments of
reconciliation as weather changes in which "o céu se fizesse
azul, o sol claro e o mar chão, por onde abríamos novamente as
velas que nos levavam às ilhas e costas mais belas do universo"
(the sky would be blue, the sun bright and the sea smooth, and
we would again unfurl our sails, and they would carry us to the
fairest islands and coasts of the universe—chap. 132). Recount-
ing the troubled phase of their marriage just before their
separation, he says that they experienced "temporais . . .
contínuos e terríveis" (storms—continuous and terrible—chap.
132), and calls the idea of Capitu's betrayal "aquela má terra
da verdade (that evil land of Truth—chap. 132). Finally, as he
reaches the most bitter part of his story, the narrator admits,
"conto aquela parte da minha vida, como um marujo contaria o
seu naufrágio" (I tell this part of my life as an old sailor recalls
his shipwreck—chap. 132).

Some of these metaphors define Bentinho and Capitu as
companion travelers, confronting together the threats of an
unsympathetic sea world. The important image of Capitu's
"olhos de ressaca," however, defines the relationship in an
entirely different way:

> Olhos de ressaca? Vá, de ressaca. É o que me dá idéia daquela
> feição nova. Traziam não sei que fluido misterioso e enérgico,
> uma força que arrastava para dentro, como a vaga que se retira
> da praia, nos dias de ressaca. Para não ser arrastado, agarrei-me
> às outras partes vizinhas, às orelhas, aos braços, aos cabelos
> espalhados pelos ombros; mas tão depressa buscava as pupilas, a
> onda que saía delas vinha crescendo, cava e escura, ameaçando
> envolver-me, puxar-me e tragar-me.

> Undertow eyes? Yes, undertow eyes. That's what they were. They
> had some mysterious and force-giving fluid that drew everything
> up into them, like a wave that moves back from the shore when
> the tide is heavy. In order not to be swept under, I grasped at
> other, neighboring parts, her ears, her arms, at her hair that was

> spread over her shoulders; but as soon as I sought the pupils of her eyes again, the wave that came from them kept growing, cavernous, dark, threatening to engulf me, to pull me, drag me into itself. (chap. 32)

Here Capitu *is* the adverse ocean itself, threatening to "envolver," "puxar," and "tragar" Bentinho. According to this important trope, she is not so much a sympathetic helper in the hero's quest as the mysterious and arduous challenge of the quest itself. Like an undertow, she exerts a strong attraction and arouses her friend's desire to approach and possess. At the same time, however, she threatens destruction, prompting him to recoil to a safer distance. The alternating reaction of approach and retreat, with its corresponding determination and frustration in Bentinho, is a wave-like pattern. As we saw in chapter 3, this oscillation is suggested by another definition of the word "ressaca"—that of the tide. The "ressaca" metaphor establishes Capitu as the complementary arbiter or agent for Bentinho's psychic rising and falling. He continually sinks and surges along a vital wave, concretely embodied in Capitu.

Capitu and the Anima Figure

Such a characterization of Capitu places her squarely within a narrative tradition involving literature, folklore, and myth. She belongs to a particular type, often called the "anima figure" according to the terminology of C. G. Jung. Since Jung's concept of the anima has little bearing on the study of literature *per se*, we will forgo Jung the psychologist and consider Jung the *typologist*, who like Freud often functioned as a kind of cataloguer of texts (including folk tales, literature, myths, dreams, and fantasies), isolating motifs and types as they proved convenient as evidence for psychological theories. Jung says that there is a considerable variety of anima characters, including types both sympathetic and antagonistic, innocent and diabolic. However, speaking of water imagery in imaginative stories, he isolates a specific narrative archetype:

> Whoever looks into the water sees his own image, but behind it living creatures soon loom up; fishes, presumably harmless dwellers of the deep—harmless, if only the lake were not haunted. They are water-beings of a peculiar sort. Sometimes a nixie gets into the fisherman's net, a female, half-human fish. Nixies are entrancing creatures:

Half drew she him,
Half sank he down
And nevermore was seen.

The nixie is an even more instinctive version of the magical feminine being I call the *anima*. She can also be a siren, melusina (mermaid), wood-nymph, Grace, or Erlking's daughter, or a lamia or succubus, who infatuates young men and sucks the life out of them.[2]

As Jung himself suggests, there are numerous variations of this narrative type. However, there appear to be certain essential characteristics that belong to all of them. They are imbued with a powerful allurement and seem to convince their pursuers that they can be caught and embraced no matter how elusive they may at times act. But they are dangerously changeable. When the exuberant male is near the point of possessing his prize, he discovers (often too late) that there is something terrible and destructive about her magical power. His reaction is one of immediate recoil; he tries, often in vain, to return to a safe distance. A few critics have already called attention to the relationship between Capitu and various archetypes or sea myths.[3] The resemblance between Capitu and the siren figure as discussed by Jung, with its connection with the sea, its magical attraction, and its destructive potential, is particularly striking.

The metaphorical equivalence between Capitu's eyes and an undertow is an economical way of transforming Capitu into a kind of nixie, while avoiding the necessity of engaging in fantastic discourse proper. It allows for displaced myth-making within the realistic setting of Rio de Janeiro. The essential qualities of the siren anima seem to be present in the passage cited earlier. Capitu's eyes are a "fluido misterioso e enérgico." Like an undertow, they possess a powerful force "que arrastava para dentro." Beholding their mysterious danger forces Bentinho to grasp desperately at surrounding features—at ears, arms, and hair—to avoid being "arrastado." Capitu is unavoidably attractive to him, yet somehow terrible.

As Capitu and Bentinho interact over time, and as Bentinho becomes increasingly frustrated at not being able to possess his beloved as completely as he needs to, the narrator emphasizes the terrible aspect of the type in his characterization. The image of Capitu's undertow eyes, weeping over Escobar's drowned body, shows horror and destruction: "Momento houve em que os olhos de Capitu fitaram o defunto, quais os da viúva, sem o pranto nem palavras desta, mas grandes e abertos, como a vaga do mar lá fora, como se quisesse tragar também o nadador da manhã" (There was a moment when Capitu's eyes gazed down at the dead man just as the widow's had, though without her weeping or any accompanying words, but great and wide like the swollen wave of the sea beyond, as if she too wished to swallow up the swimmer of that morning—chap 123). Through a subtle blending of images, this episode seems to bring to a climax the suggestiveness of Capitu's destructive capability and her tremendous attractive power. The comparison of her widely opened eyes with "a vaga do mar lá fora, como se quisesse tragar também o nadador da manhã," is the key to this figurative suggestion. Escobar has drowned in an undertow. The superimposition of that killing undertow upon Capitu's undertow eyes suggests effectively her annihilating potential. Various acts of "swallowing up" are superimposed. During the combing session, Bentinho has been swallowed up, or very nearly so, in Capitu's eyes. Surely there is a sexual suggestion in this submission.[4] As Bentinho observes his wife at Escobar's wake, he connects Escobar's disastrous drowning with Capitu's attractive power, including its sexual aspect. She becomes at this crucial moment not only mysteriously perilous, but blatantly destructive—not just alluring, but indiscriminately, cruelly unfaithful.

Though lacking the suggestiveness of ocean imagery, another recurring description of Capitu's eyes further serves to identify her with the nixie figure. José Dias remarks: "Você já reparou nos olhos dela? São assim de cigana oblíqua e dissimulada" (Did you ever notice those eyes of hers? Gypsy's eyes—oblique and sly—chap. 25). The description surely suggests evasiveness and even dishonesty. The gypsy woman is a time-honored type, imbued with mystery and possessing the ability to use subtle but convincing ploys to attract unsuspecting persons in order to steal from them.

Going beyond physical description and into the realm of action, we see that through a series of contrary actions that cause Bentinho continual exasperation, Capitu creates a reaction of alternating attraction and flight. An interesting example is Capitu's undoing of Bentinho's combing of her hair in order to hide from her mother the effect of that first kiss.

Combing Capitu's hair assumes a lyrical, nearly sacred significance to Bentinho. As mentioned in chapters 2 and 3, it is a point
of epiphany in which time is abolished. Even more significance
is attached to the session after its culminating kiss. But Capitu's
impish reaction when her mother enters the room is in direct opposition to Bentinho's worshipful enchantment:

> —Mamãe, olhe como este senhor cabeleireiro me penteou:
> Pediu-me para acabar o penteado, e fez isto. Veja que tranças!
> —Que tem? acudiu a mãe, transbordando de benevolência.
> Está muito bem, ninguém dirá que é de pessoa que não sabe
> pentear.
> —O que, mamãe? Isto? redargüiu Capitu, desfazendo as tran-
> ças. Ora mamãe.
> E com um enfadamento gracioso e voluntário que às vezes
> tinha, pegou do pente e alisou os cabelos para renovar o penteado.
> D. Fortunata chamou-lhe tonta, e disse-me que não fizesse caso,
> não era nada, maluquices da filha.

> "Mamma, see what this gentleman-hairdresser has done to my
> hair; he asked to finish combing it, and he did this. Look at the
> braids!"
> "What's wrong with them?" replied her mother kindly. "It
> looks all right, no one would guess that it had been done by
> someone who had never combed hair before."
> "What, Mamma? This?" protested Capitu as she undid the
> braids. "Oh, Mamma!"
> And with a charming air of crossness that she assumed at
> times, she took the comb and smoothed her hair and began to
> braid it over. Dona Fortunata called her silly and told me not to
> mind, that it was only her daughter's foolishness. (chap. 34)

More than a mere act of grooming, the "penteado" is a display
of love, a natural prelude to the kiss that ensues. When Capitu
undoes her hairdo, she in effect undoes the kiss as well, suggesting that neither one is very well executed or very important.
Attraction is thus followed by repulsion.

Another contradictory set of actions soon follows. Bentinho
leaves Capitu's house for his Latin lesson, but within a few
moments is back in her presence, alone, eager to "agarrar Capitu, desfazer-lhe as tranças, refazê-las e conclui-las daquela
maneira particular, boca sobre boca" (grab Capitu, undo her
braids, redo them and finish them in that particular manner,
mouth on mouth—chap. 36). But he finds Capitu in a completely
different mood—silent, oblique, distant. Instilled with bravery

after the previous encounter, he pulls her toward him. She resists by averting her bust, head, and lips, and a silent battle ensues. Then suddenly the battle is over:

> Ouvimos o ferrolho da porta que dava para o corredor interno; . . . antes que o pai acabasse de entrar, [Capitu] fez um gesto inesperado, pousou a boca na minha boca, e deu de vontade o que estava a recusar à força. Repito, a alma é cheia de mistérios.

> We heard the bolt of the door opening into the hall; . . . before her father could come into the room, [Capitu] made an unhoped for gesture, she placed her mouth on mine, and gave willingly what she had refused to yield to force. I repeat: the soul is full of mysteries. (chap. 37).

This shifting behavior is made ambiguous and mysterious by the fact that Capitu is gifted with an almost super-human capacity to control exterior expressions of her inner state of mind, and by the fact that in many cases she may feign lack of affection to hide the intentions of the lovers. The chapter called "A dissimulação" (The deceit), in which Capitu does several apparently cruel things, provides an excellent example. First, she sends Bentinho back home when he comes to her house to visit. However, she says he needs to spend his time during his weekly visits from the seminary with his mother. Later, when asked by D. Glória if Bentinho will make a good priest, she agrees with conviction. Still later, Bentinho learns that she has told D. Glória that she wants him to be the officiating priest when she gets married. After hearing about this at the dinner table, Bentinho says, "tratei de comer. Mas comi mal; estava tão contente com aquela grande dissimulação de Capitu" (I busied myself with eating. But I ate little. I was so happy over Capitu's masterpiece of deceit—chap. 65). Happy, perhaps, but there is insecurity as well. Bentinho runs to Capitu's house after dinner, seeking reassurance that she was not being cruel with her statement. Bentinho concludes, "—Você tem razão, Capitu, . . . vamos enganar toda esta gente. —Não é? disse ela com ingenuidade" ("You are right, Capitu," I concluded, "we will fool the whole bunch of them." "Won't we just?" she replied ingenuously—chap. 65).

Perhaps Bentinho's central problem in dealing with Capitu is trying to determine when she is feigning and when she is not. She is his siren image; he perceives in her the capability for destructive, arbitrary, and spiteful acts, for powerfully attractive affection, for disguising her motives. These three powers are irreconcilable for Bentinho, and therefore he sees Capitu as an unattainable being, darting about within his emotional landscape, ever evading his pursuing grasp. When he extends his arms to embrace her, he can never be sure that he will not embrace the void or a column of rock.

Within the novel, the elusive Capitu acts as a catalyst for the shifts in Bentinho's emotional state. When he feels the possibility of closeness, his spirit rises; he is optimistic, expansive, and capable. When he gets closer and discovers her terrible aspect, he shrinks back, sinking into frustration, bitterness, and despair. When these terrible images finally get the best of him, he recoils more completely and insists on separation. Jung describes the psychological characteristics of persons who repudiate the challenging relationship with an anima figure. In several respects, he seems to be identifying another narrative type, corresponding to our Dom Casmurro, "homem calado e metido consigo" (a morose, tight-lipped man withdrawn within himself—chap. 1): "After middle life, . . . permanent loss of the anima means a diminution of vitality, of flexibility, and of human kindness. The result, as a rule, is premature rigidity, crustiness, stereotypy, fanatical one-sidedness, irresponsibility and finally a childish *remolissement* with a tendency to alcohol."[5]

Bentinho's termination of the marriage relationship, with its resulting stagnation, is a reaction against the perpetual unsteadiness and ambiguity he perceives in Capitu. Her continually shifting nature, with the dangerous threat it implies, is capsulized in the "ressaca" metaphor.

Synecdoche: Capitu as a Microcosm

The image "olhos de ressaca" is at the same time more than a simple metaphor. In the context of a narrative tradition, it is a synecdoche as well. As mentioned earlier, the setting of quest narratives is often a threatening sea environment. The quest itself is a voyage through that space.[6] Within whatever medium, a quest often involves an important woman. Her love may be a kind of prize awaiting the triumphant hero at the end of the adventure. If the woman has been wronged somehow, she may symbolize the condition of necessity or loss that motivates the quest. Or, she may represent the mystery and challenge facing the hero. In any case, according to the tradition, she is a character *within* a large and encompassing space.

Dom Casmurro belongs to this narrative tradition, and the tradition belongs to *Dom Casmurro*. There is an inversion of the part for the whole and the whole for the part. Rather than creating a broad, expansive setting, the novel creates a small one. Essentially, the main setting of the novel is a household, or in its widest sense, a city. The characters do little physical traveling. But as I have pointed out, the novel depicts a great deal of travel (principally maritime) on a metaphoric level. The relationship between Bentinho and Capitu is defined as a sea voyage, and the sea is embodied within the eyes of Capitu. Thus, instead of the woman's being contained in a sea world, as would be the case in the tradition of heroic adventure stories, the sea world is contained within the woman. Encompassing and narrow space exchange places. Because of this exchange, the novel is able to be "small" on a realistic level—to be a matter of a petty protagonist and a *petite bourgeoisie*—and at the same time involve the "larger-than-life" world of myth.

We have seen that life is a sea voyage and that the voyage is contained within Capitu. We have seen that mythic adventures are often a sea voyage and that therefore a narrative tradition is contained within Capitu as well. Life, myth, and virtually every sort of global significance within the novel are capsulized within Machado's great feminine creation. Capitu is the cosmos itself.

Intertextual Travels

The metaphorical conduit to *Dom Casmurro*'s universal meaning entails journeys (life is a sea voyage) and written or performed texts (life is an opera). Not only does Capitu carry within her the great series of figurative associations involving sea travel, but she also contains those involving texts. The following passage about an encounter between Capitu and Bentinho as youths describes the girl metaphorically as a written text: "Padre futuro, estava assim diante dela como de um altar, sendo uma das faces a Epístola e a outra o Evangelho" (I future padre, thus stood before her as before an altar, and one side of her face was the Epistle and the other the Gospel—chap. 14). Describing Capitu's cheeks as parts of the Bible (which are also parts of an altar), the narrator makes her the written repository of sacred knowledge according to the Christian tradition. But her association with texts goes beyond "as escrituras" and becomes, I believe, a matter of "a escritura" or the great tradition of writing in general.[7]

One can identify various levels of intertextual reference[8] in the novel with differing degrees of relatedness or approximation to the story of Bentinho and Capitu. The level furthest removed from *Dom Casmurro* is the one I have discussed already at length—that of myth, or more specifically, the quest myth. Machado's novel abounds with displaced, ironized parallels with the quest myth. We can speak of an "intertextual" relationship between the novel and myth (in a loose sense, because myth is not actually a written text), but we cannot speak in terms of allusions because the myth is not specific enough to permit that sort of reference.

A great body of literature in the so-called Western Tradition derives from mythic narrative. *Dom Casmurro* also abounds with allusions (and now the term is appropriate) to the classics in that tradition. We find references to Homer (chaps. 17, 61, 125), Tacitus (chap. 40), Lucien (chap. 64), Cato and Plato (chap. 136), the Bible (chaps. 14, 16, 101), Dante (chaps. 32, 139), Shakespeare (chaps. 62, 72, 100, 135), Montaigne (chap. 68), and Goethe (chap. 2). We discover a particular tendency in these allusions when we note the characters referred to: Job, Achilles, Priam, Othello, Macbeth, Faust, and others. Generally, the characters are from epics or tragedies, genres in which the protagonists are defined by their greatness of character and heroism. This more specified level of allusion, then, has a close affinity with the deeper level of the quest myth. The classic works present relatively little displacement from the myth because the quality of potency and heroism in the protagonists is not substantially lost. Although in the case of *Othello* there exists a certain degree of parallelism between the narratives,[9] we would have to say that *Dom Casmurro* is not closely related to these works as a general rule. The classics seem simply to reinforce the novel's mythic underpinnings and to support its underlying heroic element.

Another European classic alluded to, but one that also belongs to the more narrow tradition of Luso-Brazilian letters, is Luís de Camões' *Os Lusíadas*. I believe it is appropriate to speak of a different level of intertextual reference here, for when a Portuguese-speaking author alludes to Camões, he is not simply referring to another classic in the general tradition of Western literature but to a national tradition.

The novel's explicit allusions to Camões are meagre, and one could hardly build a convincing argument for extensive parallels solely on that basis. In the chapter "Os braços" (Arms), where Bentinho forbids Capitu to appear in public with bare-arms, he compares the semi-transparent covering for the arms of her new dresses with Venus' diaphanous clothing in the epic poem, which she wore in her appeal on behalf of the Portuguese before Jupiter: "Levou [os braços] meio vestidos de escumilha ou não sei que, que nem cobria nem descobria inteiramente, como o cendal de Camões" (... her arms were half clothed in some filmy stuff or other, which neither covered them nor entirely discovered them, like the sendal of Camões—chap. 105). The chapter "Uma comparação" is a nostalgic gloss on Camões' lament "que nos faltam Homeros" (that we lack Homers—chap. 125). The only other reference is in the chapter "O penteado." Having just resorted to hyperbole, saying he wanted to "tecer duas tranças que pudessem envolver o infinito por um número inominável de vezes" (weave two braids that might enfold the infinite an unnameable number of times), the narrator justifies the exaggeration:

> Se isto vos parecer enfático, desgraçado leitor, é que nunca penteastes uma pequena, nunca pusestes as mãos adolescentes na jovem cabeça de uma ninfa... Uma ninfa! todo eu estou mitológico. Ainda há pouco, falando dos seus olhos de ressaca, cheguei a escrever Tétis; risquei Tétis, risquemos ninfa; digamos somente uma criatura amada, palavra que envolve todas as potências cristãs e pagãs.

> If this seems overemphatic, miserable reader, it is because you have never combed a girl's hair, never placed your adolescent hands on the youthful head of a nymph... A nymph! I am all mythology. Even before, when I was speaking of her undertow eyes, I wrote Thetis—then crossed it out. Let us also cross out nymph. Let us say only, loved creature, a word which embraces all the potencies, Christian and pagan. (chap. 33)

The passage does not *have* to be an allusion to Camões; the nymph Thetis is not the Portuguese poet's invention. Within the Brazilian or Portuguese tradition, however, the Lusitanian epic is the most accessible text making reference to the goddess.[10]

As the novel's intertextual reference enters into the realm of Luso-Brazilian literature, the degree of specificity becomes much greater. As I have shown, in *Dom Casmurro* a love story is given the metaphorical dimension of a heroic sea voyage. *Os Lusíadas* does the inverse, telling the glorious story of a nation's sea explorations on a literal level and communicating a love story on a figurative level. The two great episodes establishing *Os Lusíadas* as a metaphoric love story are the sailors' encounter with the giant Adamastor and their triumph on the "Ilha dos Amores" (Isle of Love). Interestingly, Thetis, to whom the narrator refers in *Dom Casmurro*,[11] is an integral part of the Adamastor episode. Here the giant tells of his bitter encounter with the nymph:

> Ja néscio, já da guerra desistindo,
> Ũa noite, de Dóris prometida,
> Me aparece de longe o gesto lindo
> Da branca Tétis, única, despida.
> Como doudo corri, de longe abrindo
> Os braços para aquela que era vida
> Deste corpo, e começo os olhos belos
> A lhe beijar, as faces e os cabelos.
>
> Oh! Que não sei de nojo como o conte!
> Que, crendo ter nos braços quem amava,
> Abraçado me achei cum duro monte
> De áspero mato e de espessura brava.
> Estando cum penedo fronte a fronte,
> Que eu polo rosto angélico apertava,
> Não fiquei homem, não, mas mudo e quedo
> E, junto dum penedo, outro penedo![12]

> By now confounded, and giving up the struggle,
> I receive one night, as promised by Doris,
> ‚The distant appearance, the beautiful face
> Of the white Thetis, singular, disrobed.
> As a madman I run, from a long ways opening
> My arms towards the one who is the life
> Of this life, and I begin to kiss
> Her beautiful eyes, her cheeks and her hair.
>
> Oh! But how in my anguish can I tell it?
> Behold, believing to have in my arms my beloved,
> I found myself embracing a hard mountain,
> Harsh and brutal with its thick forest.
> Being face to face with a cliff,

> Which I had taken for an angelic face,
> I became not a man, no, but dumb and silent,
> Next to a cliff, another cliff.

If according to the novel, Capitu is Thetis, then by implication Bentinho is Adamastor. In fact, Bento's entire narration is a retelling of Adamastor's bitter complaint. Both narrators tell of being betrayed by the women they loved. This woman in both cases has a "gesto lindo" and is "despida" (Capitu's arms, and presumably Thetis' entire body). In both cases, particular mention is made of the woman's "olhos," "faces," and "cabelos." The kiss is an important element in both narrations.

Both women are portrayed as an embodiment of transformation and inconsistency—Thetis in a physical sense and Capitu in a psychological sense. As a result of the betrayal, whether actual or perceived, both narrators are left rigid, silent, and ineffectual. Adamastor is "mudo e quedo," and Santiago is a "casmurro," an "homem calado e metido consigo" (chap. 1).

Adamastor's tale of betrayed love is a metaphorical prophecy to the Portuguese sailors about tragedy at sea. As chief of the nymphs, Thetis appropriately represents the ocean itself. But at least in the case of the voyage narrated, Adamastor's morbid prophecy does not come true; the explorers reach their destination unharmed. Their success is depicted metaphorically, again in terms of love, by the sensual delights of the Isle of Love. Again, we find a complementary inversion in Dom Casmurro's narration. His entails a positive prediction, that of an imagined fairy who prophesies "Tu serás feliz, Bentinho, tu vais ser feliz" (You will be happy, Bentinho, you will be happy—chap. 100). That prophecy does not come true, for the end is bitterness instead of happiness. Bentinho's unsuccessful love story is told metaphorically as a dangerous bout with the sea, and it ends with a shipwreck. In effect, his story is an ironic, backwards version of *Os Lusíadas*. Bentinho starts out at the "Ilha dos Amores," and ends up at the "Cabo das Tormentas" (Cape of Storms) with Adamastor.

Every literary work is part of a literary world, made up of other works. To a greater or lesser degree, a work must respond to the context of these other works. *Dom Casmurro* is a good example of a work that is conscious of its literary context. From beginning to end it carries on a sort of dialogue with a convention of heroic literature (or proto-literature)—from myth, to Western classics, to Luso-Brazilian literature—

responding broadly or generically to some parts of the tradition and explicitly and specifically to other parts. The novel, perhaps like any work, is itself a sort of synecdoche. It is part of a literary world, and that literary world becomes part of it.

Not coincidentally, Capitu is a kind of agent, permitting this interchange to take place. As Thetis, an example of a consecrated type of nymph-like destroyers, she becomes part of a rich literary universe. As a woman with the sea in her eyes, that same universe is part of her.

An Epistemological Quest

The rich interplay between part and whole, whole and part that exists in the novel greatly broadens the thematic reference of the work. *Dom Casmurro* goes far beyond being a novel about a domestic misunderstanding. The household is an entire universe, and Bentinho's attempt to fathom his partner's heart is Man's attempt to achieve an understanding of the cosmos. The chapter "A ópera" (The opera), which is a kind of cosmogony, must seem like an anomaly unless we recognize this universal dimension in the novel.[13] Bentinho's bitter evaluation of his wife is not just a condemnation of one individual; it is a worldview. According to that view, not only did his wife betray him, but destiny—indeed the entire universe—betrayed him also: ". . . quis o destino que acabassem juntando-se e enganando-me" (. . . destiny willed that they should join together and deceive me—chap. 148).

One of the marks of modern tales is that there are far fewer physical monsters to deal with. But although a quest fraught with physical dangers may be a thing of the past, there is more and more room for an epistemological quest. Bentinho's life is such a search. Ultimately, he ends that quest by deciding that Capitu and life have wronged him. Ironically, his decision may or may not be valid in the mind of the reader. The question of Capitu's guilt or innocence remains open.[14] The abiding ambiguity of *Dom Casmurro* transfers the epistemological quest from Bentinho to the reader. Bentinho reaches a conclusion, but the earnest reader cannot. The enigma of Capitu becomes the enigma of the novel. Those undertow eyes, with their plurivalent dangers and cross-currents, engulf a literary and mythic tradition, a mysterious cosmos, and ultimately even the novel *Dom Casmurro*.

CHAPTER SIX

Symbols of Salvation

In chapter 2, I suggested that far beneath the surface of appearances the protagonist, Bentinho, in a considerably disguised and ironic manner, is like a mythic hero engaged in a fight to the death with a powerful dragon. Bentinho's dragon, rather than some concrete monstrosity, is an even more formidable devourer—time. I attempted to demonstrate that in his drive to abolish time, Bentinho displays in several respects what Mircea Eliade and others call a primitive mentality.

The present chapter corroborates that our protagonist's behavior and attitudes are mythic and primitive and that consequently the novel has a significant mythic dimension. In the novel, myth provides an underlying system which helps make seemingly random motifs comprehensible. I wish to demonstrate this by analyzing one specific aspect—the recourse to magical substances in order to restore health or vitality.

More Primitivism: Magic and Cures

The myth of the hero's quest usually involves the motif of the cure. It often begins with a debilitating *malaise* in the hero's community or surroundings which makes it necessary for him to embark upon a restorative adventure. After succeeding in numerous crucial trials, the hero returns carrying an elixir which revitalizes his community.[1] Bentinho's destiny and behavior in the novel likewise involve cures. His birth is in itself a sort of cure for his mother, D. Glória, whose first child was born dead and who felt it necessary to make a special promise to God to overcome her barrenness. That promise, of course, was to rear her son to become a priest (chap. 11). Coincidentally, the Portuguese title "cura" (priest) suggests the connection between D. Glória's surmounted barrenness and Bentinho's priestly destiny. Bentinho comes to have other ideas for his future and succeeds in escaping from his mother's promise. However, he continues throughout his life to seek and to attempt to impart cures. Having lost his religious faith and priestly vocation, he searches for remedies not in God, but in secular rituals and quasi-magical enchantments. These are disguised in the trappings of modern life but retain a primitive essence. Instead of becoming an orthodox "cura," Santiago becomes a sort of modernized medicine man or "curandeiro."

During the first part of his life, before he becomes a "casmurro," the protagonist finds his remedy for worldly ills in his relationship with Capitu, that is, in loving. Summing up that period of his life, he gives advice to younger men which amounts to a sort of prescription or cure: "Amai, rapazes! e, principalmente, amai moças lindas e graciosas; elas dão remédio ao mal, aroma ao infecto, trocam a morte pela vida... Amai, rapazes!" (Love, lads! and, above all, love beautiful, spirited girls. They have a remedy for ills, fragrance to sweeten a stench; for death they give you life.... Love, lads, love!—chap. 86). Bentinho, of course, does not take his own medicine. Convinced that Capitu has betrayed him, he repudiates the cure of loving and must seek other antidotes.

The Book as an Elixir

Of these treatments, one of the most significant and most often used is that of books. In the novel, books seem to take on a magical significance as a restorer of life. Quite often, when the protagonist has regressed into melancholy, discouragement, or discomfiture, or when he feels the need for special powers for some challenging task, he seems to grasp for books as a kind of boon. These books indeed seem to have a vitalizing effect, although always for a shorter period than Bentinho would like.

Although Santiago is both a reader and a writer, he has a concrete and functional approach to books. In this respect, he shares the characteristics of members of primitive, illiterate societies. A brief anecdote will, I hope, help illustrate my point. One day a book salesman knocked at a woman's door. "I have here," he said, "a book that you will enjoy a great deal." "Sorry," the woman said, "but I don't know how to read." The salesman then replied, "But surely your children will be interested." The woman informed the man that she had no children. "But how about your husband?" The woman informed him that she was not married, and that the only other being in her household was a cat. The salesman scratched his head a moment, and said, "You still need to buy this book, because when that cat of yours steals food from the table, you're going to need a book to throw at it." The woman easily saw his point, agreed completely, and bought the book.

The man in this story succeeded in making a sale because he could communicate with his customer on her level. Realizing she was illiterate, he sold the book by telling her what she could *do with* it, instead of what she could *learn from* it. Bento Santiago is in some ways quite similar to this woman. He tends to react to books almost like a person who does not read, viewing them as something with which to accomplish a concrete task rather than as a source of abstract information.

For example, Bento explains in the second chapter how he first got the idea to write a book; he was bored, and writing a book would be a cure for his condition: "Ora, como tudo cansa, esta monotonia acabou por exaurir-me também. Quis variar, e lembrou-me escrever um livro" (But as everything wearies one, this monotony too finally exhausted me. I wanted change. What if I wrote a book?—chap. 2). The topic he chooses is "uma *História dos subúrbios*" (a *History of the Suburbs*—chap. 2). Such a topic is deliberately useless and trivial, since the book's function is not to inform other readers but rather to serve as a remedy for its writer.

For another example, let us consider the books depicted in the chapter "Os vermes" (The worms—chap. 17). The narrator has just described the rising and falling fortunes of his former neighbor and father-in-law, Pádua. In summary, he quotes a scripture he heard as a young boy from Padre Cabral, who was also commenting on Pádua: "Não desprezes a correção do Senhor; Ele fere e cura" (Despise not the chastening of the

Almighty; He woundeth and He maketh whole—chap. 16).
Then, the narrator says:

> "Ele fere e cura!" Quando, mais tarde, vim a saber que a lança
> de Aquiles também curou uma ferida que fez, tive tais ou quais
> veleidades de escrever uma dissertação a este propósito. Cheguei
> a pegar em livros velhos, livros mortos, livros enterrados, a
> abri-los, a compará-los, catando o texto e o sentido, para achar a
> origem comum do oráculo pagão e do pensamento israelita.

> "He woundeth and He maketh whole!" Later, when I came to
> know that the lance of Achilles also cured the wound it made, I
> had a fleeting desire to write a dissertation on this problem. I
> went so far as to pick up old books, dead books, buried books,
> open them, compare them, in order to track down the text and the
> meaning, and discover the common origin of the pagan oracle
> and the Israelite thought. (chap. 17)

The phrase "mais tarde" signals change and seems to refer to
the period of time in which Bentinho has become "Dom Casmurro," when he has ceased to have faith in loving as a cure. We
have the impression that the writing of a dissertation on such
an obscure and trivial topic is a distraction for someone who no
longer has anything meaningful to do. We are reminded of his
project to write a history of the suburbs. Writing "uma disser-
tação" seems to be, in effect, another cure for boredom. The book
here does not simply say something, it *does* something. The
narrator has "veleidades," or a brief resurgence of will. In a
greatly displaced manner, he experiences the mythic call to
adventure and begins to embark upon a quest, displaced to a
search, displaced to research. His grasping hold of "livros vel-
hos, livros mortos, livros enterrados, a abri-los, a compará-los,
catando o texto e o sentido" suggests a coming to life or a
resurrection. It is appropriate that this bookish rebirth is literally connected, through a scriptural passage, with the idea of
a cure. The notion of a book, and Bentinho's subsequent recourse to books, seem in fact to bring about a momentary cure
of his "casmurrice." But the boon of the books is brief indeed. No
sooner does he open the books, than the bookworms, with their
nihilistic "nós não sabemos absolutamente nada dos textos que
roemos" (we know absolutely nothing of the texts we gnaw—
chap. 17), return him to his state of acquiescence.

We find another example of the power of a book to restore
vitality in the *Panegírico de Santa Mônica*. A gift from a former
colleague from the seminary, the *Panegírico* recovers life through
memory:

Tudo me ia repetindo o diabo do opúsculo, com as suas letras velhas e citações latinas. Vi sair daquelas folhas muitos perfis de seminaristas. . . . Quantas outras caras me fitavam das páginas frias do *Panegírico*! Não, não eram frias; traziam o calor da juventude nascente, o calor do passado, o meu próprio calor. Queria lê-las outra vez, e lograva entender algum texto, tão recente como no primeiro dia, ainda que mais breve. Era um encanto ir por ele; às vezes, inconscientemente, dobrava a folha como se estivesse lendo de verdade; creio que era quando os olhos me caíam na palavra do fim da página, e a mão, acostumada a ajudá-los, fazia o seu ofício...

All this the devil of a little book kept telling me, with its old style type and Latin quotations. I saw rise from those leaves many a seminarist profile. . . . How many other faces stared up at me from the cold pages of the *Panegyric*! No, they were not cold. They bore the warmth of budding youth, the warmth of the past, my own warmth. I wanted to reread them; here and there I caught the meaning of the text; it seemed as fresh to me as on the first day, though more brief. The little book cast a spell: at times, unconsciously, I turned the page as if I were actually reading. And then . . . I believe that it was when my eyes fell on the last word on the page, and my hand, accustomed to assist them, did its office... (chap. 56)

The language of this passage is one of magic and "encanto." The book's pages make people come to life and restore the heat of youthful energy. It is important to note that the enchanting power of the *Panegírico* has nothing to do with reading in the normal sense of gaining information. The work's written language seems in itself unimportant, since Bentinho is not "lendo de verdade." Rather than exerting power through poetic evocation or literary imagery in the traditional sense, the book possesses a more fetishistic power, arising from its status as a physical object. We have the impression that merely holding the book is all that is necessary for the spell of rejuvenating remembrance. But as with the case of research on cures, we detect a reversal in the book's effect upon Bentinho. At first it causes a blossoming, as the protagonist relives experiences of youth and optimism. The same little book, however, leads him to reexperience the beginnings of his jealousy and disillusionment and naturally leads to a corruption of the initially positive experience.

Normally ineffectual and indecisive, Bentinho resorts to books when he needs special strength for decisive action. Such is the case when he resolves to kill himself in the depths of bitterness over his wife's supposed infidelity. Before dissolving poison in his coffee, Bentinho remembers that "Catão, antes de se mater, leu e releu um livro de Platão" (Cato, before he killed himself, read and reread a book of Plato—chap. 136). Not having any work of Plato at hand, he finds a volume of Plutarch that narrates the life of Cato and reads that book. His actions are first of all understandable within the context of ritual. Possessing a primitive mentality, Bentinho is against linear time and against all that is modern. He desires to return to antiquity, to the point of origin, and therefore imitates a heroic model from early times in his attempt to kill himself. But his actions are also significant in their tendency toward magic and fetishism. He is faced with a formidable challenge requiring resolution and strength and seems to grasp a book in the belief that it will be a magical balm, providing him the power to carry out his plan. He says, ". . . tinha necessidade de incutir em mim a coragem dele [de Catão], assim como ele precisara dos sentimentos do filósofo, para intrepidamente morrer" (I had to arouse in myself the same courage, just as he [Cato] had required the thoughts of the philosopher to die intrepidly—chap. 136). Here again, the function of the book is primarily *doing* rather than saying. As with the other cases, the power bestowed by the book is temporary and insufficient. Bentinho manages to dissolve the poison but is unable to swallow it.

The book-magic discussed so far seems to fall within the category of what Sir James Frazer calls "contagious magic," that is, the exchange of causes or effects through objects that are or have been associated.[2] We might also call it "magic by metonymy." Bento reaches for old books that may have discussed ancient cures. The metonymic confusion of treatise and subject matter gives the books themselves temporary curative powers which cause the protagonist to feel dynamic and willful. The *Panegírico*, through association with its author, with the seminary, and with a youthful period in Santiago's life, restores the protagonist to a momentary impression of newness and vitality. The book by Plutarch, being in part about Cato, starts to give Bentinho some of the determination and resolve of Cato.

There remains another important case of book enchantment— the case of *Dom Casmurro* itself. In the chapter entitled "Do livro" (The book), the narrator explains that his purpose in having written the book was to restore his youth. "Deste modo, viverei o que vivi" (In this way I will live what I have lived—chap. 2), he says. As with the other examples, there is an element of contagious magic in this behavior. The book will be *about* a period of optimism, health, and energy; therefore, the book will, through contagion, restore some of those qualities to the hand and mind that produce it. At the same time we find aspects of another type of magic in the writing of this memoir. Called by Frazer homeopathic or imitative magic,[3] this sort has to do with the exchange of influence or effect between a primary object and secondary replica. For example, one mutilates a doll made in imitation of a particular person and causes injury to that person.

An excellent example of this type of magical behavior is found in Santiago's construction of a replica of his childhood home, with a curative purpose, to "atar as duas pontas da vida, e restaurar na velhice a adolecência" (tie together the two ends of my life, to restore adolescence in old age—chap. 2). For Bento, the writing of his memoirs and the reconstruction of the house are parallel acts. He never discusses the function of one without mentioning the other (chaps. 2, 64). While the book as an object is not a physical replica of anything from a person's youth except books themselves, books participate in a long mimetic tradition in which it is agreed through convention that words can be imitations of objects from life. In this sense the memoir participates in imitative as well as contagious magic.

That primitive recourse to an elixir is not without its effect. The idea of writing a book gives Santiago a pulse of new life. He has depicted himself as a morose, taciturn, hermit of a man (chap. 1), but as a narrator, especially in the first part of the book, he is the direct opposite. He is generally loquacious and exuberant and communicates to the point of confession. The book does in fact seem to restore life to our normally reticent protagonist. But the book's restorative powers never go far enough. As soon as the narration takes him to the bitter phase of his life, the narrator begins to run out of "paper" and will to narrate. He acknowledges that the latter phase of his account, which ought to constitute an entire half of the book, will be compressed instead into a much smaller portion (chap. 97). By the time he finishes, he is every bit the "casmurro" he was when he started.

His final utterance in the novel is "Vamos à *História dos suburbios*" (On to the *History of the Suburbs*). With this imperative he returns to the first book he mentioned. We recall that the suburban history is the book he originally intended to write to cure his boredom before the idea of a memoir occurred to him. He has tried producing one book as a salve for his ills and has found that as an elixir it is incapable of sustained effect. But in an absurdly determined manner, reminiscent of the circularity of Sisyphus,[4] he seems disposed to try *ad infinitum* the same disappointing medicine.

Money as a Modern Talisman

Money is another frequently mentioned substance which is used in an irrational way to try to restore vitality. A magical substance might be defined as one with abnormal capabilities. It is a bit hard to discuss money as such a substance, since in modern society the normal powers of money are so great that there is very little left for the realm of magic. But it is a commonplace that there are still some things money cannot buy, such as love or immortality. In the novel, money is used as a sort of primitive talisman to try to acquire these very things.

Money has a few important characteristics that make it an appropriate symbol, mediating between the modern context and the mythic context in *Dom Casmurro*. Economists speak of its three essential properties.[5] First, it is a medium of exchange. As a concrete object, it facilitates commerce and trade, bringing parties together in a "meeting of the minds." Money is used in this way in the novel; however, it also becomes a medium for more ineffable exchanges, such as love. Second, money is a standard of value, a gauge of the degree to which things are wanted and needed. In *Dom Casmurro*, it is used to place value upon several commodities and at the same time to show by analogy the value attached to priceless substances such as esteem, peace of mind, and health. Thirdly, money is a repository of wealth, allowing for its continuation and preservation through time. The novel shows money being used in this material fashion but also employs it to suggest conserving against time the immeasurable wealth of life itself. In Machado's novel, money comes into play both literally and figuratively. In either case, its symbolism is supercharged: it becomes a matter of life and death.

As I mentioned earlier, Bentinho's birth can be seen as a kind of cure. However, it is a cure with serious side effects. Another way of looking at the problem is through the figurative lens of money. As a young married couple, Bentinho's parents are happy and prosperous. The narrator describes their felicity metaphorically, in terms of a grand prize in the lottery. Referring to a portrait of his parents, he concludes, "O que se lê na cara de ambos é que, se a felicidade conjugal pode ser comparada à sorte grande, eles a tiraram no bilhete comprado de sociedade" (What you read in the face of both is that if conjugal felicity can be compared to the grand prize in a lottery, they had won it with the ticket they purchased together—chap. 7). While their material wealth continues to grow, their "prize" of happiness turns to scarcity because of barrenness. After D. Glória has a stillborn child, she promises God that if given a son she will make him a priest. In a figurative sense, that promise puts her heavily in debt:

> Um dos aforismos de Franklin é que, para quem tem de pagar na Páscoa, a Quaresma é curta. A nossa quaresma não foi mais longa que as outras, e minha mãe, posto me mandasse ensinar latim e doutrina, começou a adiar a minha entrada no seminário. É o que se chama, comercialmente falando, reformar uma letra. O credor era arquimilionário, não dependia daquela quantia para comer, e consentiu nas transferências de pagamento, sem sequer agravar a taxa do juro. Um dia, porém, um dos familiares que serviam de endossantes da letra, falou da necessidade de entregar o preço ajustado; está num dos capítulos primeiros. Minha mãe concordou e recolhi-me a S. José.
>
> One of the aphorisms of Franklin states that for him who must pay at Easter, Lent is short. Our Lent was no longer than the others, and my mother, while she had me taught Latin and Religion, began to defer the day of my entering the seminary. It is what is called, commercially speaking, "extending a note." The Creditor was a multimillionaire; He was not dependent upon payment in order to eat, and consented to postponements without even increasing the rate of interest. One day, however, one of the friends who had endorsed the note spoke of the necessity of paying the promised sum: it is in one of the first chapters. My mother agreed and I withdrew into São José. (chap. 80)

So D. Glória's tardiness in fulfilling her promise is a sort of second mortgage. Bentinho's eventual release from his mother's promise is also the result of refinancing—this time an even more clever one, involving a kind of monetary exchange. D. Glória sponsors an orphan in the seminary who accepts the vows in Bentinho's stead. In other words, she pays off her figurative debt in literal currency.

Bentinho's use of money has similar extra-commercial associations. He seems to confide in a kind of magical power in money, when as a boy he gives a couple of coins to a beggar, thinks of Capitu, and asks the beggar to pray to God so that all his desires might be satisfied (chap. 27). As he and Capitu are trying to devise a plan to escape his mother's obligation, he buys two *cocadas* from a passing vendor. In chapter 2, I discussed in some detail the idea that the *cocadas* suggest communion to Bentinho, both in a religious and an amorous sense, since candies served as the host when he and the girl played "mass." The *cocadas* or some other candy were also the object of a selling game in which the two entertained themselves, "rindo, saltando, trocando os papéis, . . . ora vendendo, ora comprando um doce ausente" (laughing, jumping and exchanging roles . . . now selling, now buying a sweet that was not there—chap. 18). Bentinho could just as easily consider this game a sort of "communion" as the liturgical play, for both involve being together in enjoyable circumstances in a type of cooperative exchange. When Bentinho buys coconut candy to share with Capitu, he is again attempting to buy, as if by magic, the return of loving closeness.

The fulfillment of Bentinho's desires, like the fulfillment of his mother's, means incurring a heavy debt through a contract with or promise to God, who is "um Rothschild muito mais humano" (a Rothschild, only much more human—chap. 69). In exchange for being absolved from D. Glória's promise, the boy pledges to recite a thousand Paternosters and a thousand Hail Marys. He explains that the reason for such a large sum is that he is already behind in complying with promises for previous blessings and intends with the two thousand prayers to "pay up" for everything:

> Mil, mil, mil. Era preciso uma soma que pagasse os atrasados todos. Deus podia muito bem, irritado com os esquecimentos, negar-se a ouvir-me sem muito dinheiro. . . . Cogitei muito no modo de resgatar a dívida espiritual. Não achava outra espécie em que, mediante a intenção, tudo se comprisse, fechando a escrituração da minha consciência moral sem *deficit*.

Thousand, thousand, thousand! I needed a sum that would pay all the arrears. God might very well be irritated with my forgetfulness and refuse to hear me without a promise of big money. . . . I cogitated deeply on how to wipe out my spiritual debt. I found no other specie in which, with due consideration for my wish, the whole could be paid and the books of my conscience closed without deficit. (chap. 20)

Of course all this banking discourse involves not some priced commodity but a priceless one—Bentinho's soul. He makes this explicit when he explains that he could have negotiated the contract by having a hundred masses said but that involvement in so many masses would be almost the same as being a priest: "As missas eram numerosas, podiam empenhar-me outra vez a alma" (The Masses would be numerous; they might once more mortgage my soul—chap. 20).

As in the case of his mother, Bentinho's happiness is described in terms of a lottery. He has a dream which ironically repeats his future father-in-law's experience with the lottery. Pádua, although earning a very modest income, was able to buy the house next to the Santiagos because he won the grand prize in a lottery (chap. 16). In Bentinho's dream, however, Pádua's ticket is a loser. Capitu's father complains that "provavelmente a roda andara mal; era impossível que não devesse ter a sorte grande. Enquanto ele falava, Capitu dava-me com os olhos todas as sortes grandes e pequenas. A maior destas devia ser dada com a boca" (probably the wheel had broken down; it was impossible that it should not have won the grand prize. While he was speaking, Capitu, with her eyes, was giving me all the prizes, great and small. The greatest of these ought to be given with the mouth—chap. 63). Both figuratively and literally, Bentinho attributes to money an almost magical power. For him it buys what money cannot normally buy. José Dias, suggesting a visit to the pope to request absolution for Bentinho, offers a cliché that sums up the attitude that money can buy happiness: "Quem tem boca vai a Roma, e boca no nosso caso é a moeda" (He who has a tongue goes to Rome, the tongue in our case is cash—chap. 95).

The innocent, hopeful period of Bentinho and Capitu's relationship is frequently characterized by financial scarcity. The cry of the street vendor of coconut candy,

Chora, menina, chora,
Chora, porque não tem
Vintém

Cry, little girl, cry,
Cry 'cause you haven't any
Penny (chap. 17),

heard when the youths intensely shared their hopes, suggests
their candid desires and frustrations in monetary terms.

Before departure from the seminary and before Bentinho
and Capitu's marriage, the protagonists are portrayed as
debtors, trying to pay off a formidable obligation. After the
marriage, the debt appears to have been satisfied in full and
the protagonists are in the contrary position of being savers
and paying cash in advance for their spiritual transactions.

The narrator points out this inversion as he tells of his and
Capitu's impatience for a baby: "Não vinha. Capitu pedia-o em
suas orações, eu mais de uma vez dava por mim a rezar e a
pedi-lo. Já não era como em criança; agora pagava antecipa-
damente, como os aluguéis da casa" (It did not come. Capitu
asked for it in her prayers. More than once I caught myself
saying prayers and asking for it. It was no longer as it had been
when I was a child; now, I paid in advance, like house rent—
chap. 104). Besides the saver/debtor inversion, there begins to
be an ironic reversal in the meaning of money. According to
John Kenneth Galbraith, "Most things in life—automobiles,
mistresses, cancer—are important only to those who have
them. Money, in contrast, is equally important to those who
have it and those who don't."[6] He might have added that while
the importance of money is equal to the "haves" and "have-
nots," the meaning they attach to it may be quite different.
Bentinho is a case in point. Before his marriage he is, figuratively speaking, in hock. Yet money symbolizes his hopes for
happiness. After marriage, his debts are paid but the money he
now possesses begins to acquire the associations of bitterness
and anxiety.

The previous quotation about the desire for a child, in which
Bentinho puts down cash without being sure of receiving
something in return, exemplifies this new ironic meaning
attached to money. The chapter "Dez Libras Esterlinas" (Ten
Pounds Sterling) is another good example. In this chapter
Capitu becomes distracted while Bentinho is teaching her
about the stars. Capitu explains that she was mentally review-

ing the calculations of a transaction she had carried out earlier that day. She had bought ten pounds sterling with savings from her allowance:

—Tudo isto?
—Não é muito, dez libras só; é o que a avarenta de sua mulher pôde arranjar, em alguns meses, concluiu fazendo tinir o ouro na mão.
—Quem foi o corretor?
—O seu amigo Escobar.
—Como é que ele não me disse nada?
—Foi hoje mesmo.
—Ele esteve cá?
—Pouco antes de você chegar; eu não disse para que você não desconfiasse.

"All this?"
"It's not much, just ten pounds. It's what your miser of a wife could save up in several months," she concluded, making the gold tinkle in her hand.
"Who was the broker?"
"Your friend Escobar."
"How is it he didn't say anything to me?"
"It was only today."
"He was here?"
"A little before you came home. I didn't mention it for fear you might suspect something. (chap. 106)

On the surface this episode seems to be a joyful occasion. It appears to show that Capitu is a conscientious homemaker and eager to economize and please her husband (promoting domestic stability). Her purchase of the pounds sterling is a wise financial move, transferring a relatively unsteady currency into a much more dependable one (promoting financial stability). It seems pleasing to Bentinho's essentially conservative nature, for a hedge against inflation is after all a hedge against the vicissitudes of change (promoting temporal stability). The narrator says he wanted to "gastar o dobro do ouro em algum presente comemorativo" (squander double the amount of the gold on some commemorative present—chap. 106).

However, in ironic contrast to these happy appearances, which are consistent with the positive meaning of money in the first part of the novel, the transaction carries some very negative meanings and is responsible for inciting Bentinho's jealousy. Capitu has done something behind her husband's back, including admitting Escobar to the house in his absence.

As indicated earlier, the make-believe exchange of money between Bentinho and Capitu as children had amorous overtones for Bentinho. It would not be unreasonable for the real-life exchange between Capitu and Escobar to carry those same overtones. There is perhaps a sexual suggestiveness to the transaction which foreshadows Bentinho's bitter accusation of his wife. The husband has been "paying" in order to have a child. The wife may in a sense get a "payment" in a more potent currency from someone else.[7]

Married and prosperous, Bentinho is perhaps unconsciously nostalgic for the period of his life when he saw himself as a debtor. His transcription and sentimental repetition (chap. 110) of the coconut candy vendor's song (chap. 18), plus his promise never to forget the song (chap. 114), seem to show his longing for the innocent happiness of "poverty."

Near the culmination of Bentinho's dark suspicion, he buys poison to kill himself. He refers to that purchase euphemistically as a large bank deposit: "A farmácia faliu, é verdade; o dono fez-se banqueiro, e o banco prospera" (The pharmacy went broke, it is true; the owner became a banker and the bank prospers—chap. 134). Again we see that Bentinho has changed from debt to opulence but that his money now buys not vitality and love, but the opposite. He resorts again to the image of the lottery, this time with an ironic and contrary meaning: "Quando me achei com a morte no bolso senti tamanha alegria como se acabasse de tirar a sorte grande, ou ainda maior, porque o prêmio da loteria gasta-se, e a morte não se gasta" (When I found myself with death in my pocket I felt as if I had just drawn the grand prize—no, greater joy; for a lottery prize dribbles away, but death does not—chap. 134).

When Ezequiel is a young man, he comes from Europe to visit Santiago and after a while asks him to supply the money for him to travel to the Near East on an archeological expedition. In narrating his gift to Ezequiel, Dom Casmurro makes explicit his ironic perception of the exchange between betrayer and betrayed which was only hinted at in the episode of the pounds sterling: "Prometi-lhe recursos, e dei-lhe logo os primeiros dinheiros precisos. Comigo disse que uma das conseqüências dos amores furtivos do pai era pagar eu as arqueologias do filho; antes pegasse a lepra" (I promised to furnish the resources, and gave him then and there an advance on the money needed. I told myself that one of the consequences of the stolen love of the father was that I gave money for the son's archeology. I'd rather have given him leprosy—chap. 145). Santiago seems more than happy to give Ezequiel the money for the trip and not only because he would prefer not to have him around. There is something of a curse in the gift.[8] Casmurro hands over the funds, hoping at the same time that the young man will get leprosy and die.

This perverse money-magic is diametrically opposed in its intentions to what we observed in the beginning of the work. As a boy, Bentinho gives alms to a beggar in the fervent hope that doing so will save his soul from the purgatory of a promise and assure life and love. As an aging man, he gives money to another sort of "beggar," this time with a wish of damnation. Both wishes are granted, but not to the same extent. Money in fact is able to buy Bentinho and Capitu the vitality and communion they so desire. However, that boon, like the lottery prize, "gasta-se." Money also seems able to effect the morbid curse upon Ezequiel, since he dies during his travels, although not from leprosy (chap. 146). The curse is more powerful than the cure because "a morte não se gasta."

Symbolic Irony: Books, Money, and Modernity

In Bento Santiago's adherence to the mentality of fetishism, his choice of books and money as remedies is highly ironic. Magical minds tend to be *bookless* minds. As numerous social scientists and critics have pointed out, magical thought thrives upon orality. The advent of literacy signals the decline of myth and magic and the birth of modern, advanced culture.[9] In this light, the narrator's obsessive recourse to books as a vitalizing escape from contemporary life is self-defeating. Money is also an essential feature of modernity; the more current and developed the society, the more intricate and developed is its monetary system. Primitive societies tend to be *moneyless*, more self-sufficient or reliant upon barter than dependent upon the complex trade networks that money makes possible.[10] Santiago chooses as his elixirs against modern times the very symbols of the modern world. This selection seems similar to trying to put out a fire by pouring fuel on it. Rather than escaping from modernity, the book-bound Santiago becomes all the more its prisoner.

Essence or Absence?

In chapter 1, I introduced the so-called four major tropes—metaphor, metonymy, synecdoche, and irony—as a set of "transformational rules" capable of effecting the displacement from myth to modern, realistic fiction. Much of my subsequent discussion was an attempt to identify the function of these tropes as elements permitting a distant correspondence between *Dom Casmurro* and the quest myth.

There is a polarity to these four figurative devices. Metaphor stands at one extreme, emphasizing sameness. Where metaphor predominates in the novel, a greater degree of approximation to myth is possible. The protagonist is given heroic dimensions and takes on aspects of equivalence with powerful mythic prototypes. The figure of irony stands at the other extreme and emphasizes difference. Ironic discourse increases the distance between myth and *Dom Casmurro*, as it calls attention to Bentinho's lack of heroic capacity. Metonymy and synecdoche are somewhere in the middle of this polarity and seem in their function to achieve a relative balance of difference and similarity.[1]

While all the tropes are at play to some degree in the mythic underpinnings of the novel, the ones to which I have devoted most of my attention are metaphor and irony. I believe this is no accident. *Dom Casmurro* establishes a polarity between metaphoric, mythic discourse, through which the narrator ties himself to timeless archetypes, and ironic discourse in which he takes account of an arbitrary, ever-changing modernity. It is also no accident that all my chapters have ended with a discussion of irony. Self-conscious, confessional, and intelligent narrator that he is, Santiago is more than willing to chronicle a bitter evaluation of his own impotent entrapment within the inhospitable contemporary world. He does this increasingly as he reaches the end of the book. Structurally, the novel ends with an ironic inversion of the quest pattern.

This final note of irony would seem to place *Dom Casmurro* squarely within the general tendency of modern literature, away from heroes toward anti-heroes, and away from the idealism of essences toward the pessimism of relativity and absurd quests. However, I wonder whether *Dom Casmurro* can be classified that simply. Bentinho clearly does not conform to the archetype by which he initially defines himself. The world to which he belongs is obviously far removed from an ideal isle of dreams. But does the ironic revelation of such a dissonance call for a negation of essences? In reality, both the concept of essences and that of relativity are subjected to the doubting scrutiny of irony.

One way the novel accomplishes this standoff is by making its narrator's acknowledgment of relativity a dogmatic one. Throughout the novel, Bentinho is an essentialist. As a protagonist in the novel's story, he consistently attempts to define himself within a patriarchal system which idealizes heroic models and authoritarian domination as a way of solving problems. As a narrator, Santiago frequently resorts to heroic language to describe himself. Yet it is evident both to the reader and to the narrator himself that reality is far removed from this idealized mythic essence. This recognition, however, does not constitute the narrator's abandonment of essences but rather the paradoxical espousal of a negative essentialism.

He portrays Capitu as the embodiment of this overturned essence. According to him, she is a metamorphosing nymph— fluid, unfaithful, and arbitrary. Her undertow eyes seem to symbolize the abyss of absence.[2] In addition, Capitu is a microcosm for the entire world; therefore, Santiago's global view confirms the same relativistic inconstancy. But the narrator, still maintaining a vestige of heroic zeal, goes so far in asserting this relativity that he essentializes it. The last chapter's final condemnation of Capitu illustrates:

> O resto é saber se a Capitu da Praia da Glória já estava dentro da de Mata-cavalos, ou se esta foi mudada naquela por efeito de algum caso incidente. Jesus, filho de Sirach, se soubesse dos meus primeiros ciúmes, dir-me-ia, como no seu cap. ix, vers. 1: "Não tenhas ciúmes de tua mulher para que ela não se meta a enganar-te com a malícia que aprender de ti". Mas eu creio que não, e tu concordarás comigo; se te lembras bem da Capitu menina, hás de reconhecer que uma estava dentro da outra, como a fruta dentro da casca.
> E bem, qualquer que seja a solução, uma cousa fica, e é a suma das sumas, ou o resto dos restos, a saber, que a minha primeira amiga e o meu maior amigo, tão extremosos ambos e tão queridos também, quis o destino que acabassem juntando-se e enganando-me.

> What remains is to discover whether the Capitu of Gloria was already within the Capitu of Matacavallos, or if this one was changed into the other as the result of some incidental fact. If Jesus, son of Sirach, had known of my first fits of jealousy, he would have said to me, as in his Ch. IX, vs. 1: "Be not jealous of thy wife lest she set herself to deceive thee with the malice that she learnt from thee." But I do not believe it was so, and you will agree with me. If you remember Capitu the child, you will have to recognize that one was within the other, like the fruit within its rind.
> Well, whatever may be the solution, one thing remains and it is the sum of sums, the rest of the residuum, to wit, that my first love and my greatest friend, both so loving me, both so loved— destiny willed that they should join together and deceive me. (chap. 148)

The final words of the novel are an assertion about the essence of Capitu. Her betraying nature, Santiago says, is at her very core, "como a fruta dentro da casca." Extrapolating from his experience with Capitu, he makes an indictment against destiny itself: "quis o destino que acabassem juntando-se e enganando-me." His concluding pronouncement then is not just a complaint about his wife, it is a world view. We see that Casmurro does not just admit the apparent reality of a world devoid of essences, he paradoxically condemns modern relativity as something destined and therefore in itself essential. Because it is dogmatically asserted, the idea of relativity is ironically called into question. Because the lone survivor of all essences is relativity, the idea of essences is likewise placed in doubt.

One of my "conclusions," then, is that while the novel is about epistemology, it is difficult if not impossible to derive epistemological conclusions from *Dom Casmurro*. The narrator is guilty of twisted logic and concludes by asserting an absolutist and an anti-absolutist position at the same time.

Santiago's advocacy of essentials is directly tied to his desire for Capitu to be true and faithful. By his own admission, he is an "enganado." Because of this "engano" he makes a case for relativity, tied to Capitu's unfaithfulness. Yet ironically, the very case he presents has a very relative validity. We can see the possibility of Capitu's fidelity behind all his accusing evidence. Whatever philosophy our narrator might advance must be doubted, therefore, because his supporting evidence is based on Capitu, and whether he is right or wrong about her, he is "enganado."

Another "conclusion" is that deriving any sort of ideological conclusion is equally problematic. The narrator's quest to abolish time with his return to primitive heroic archetypes and his metaphoric reification of woman is identifiable with an ideology that eschews progress and attempts to legitimize domination and repression.[3] One could identify this as the ideology of the novel. But it is difficult to do so when we remember that one of the possible definitions of "casmurro" is "wrong-headed";[4] this reactionary view is subject to irony. What about Capitu's rebellion against such patriarchal domination? That would seem to suggest a contrary ideology, favoring the principle of liberty and equality and attacking oppressive traditions and social roles. The novel seems to suggest this more radical ideology, but it appears to undercut it at the same time. If she is a faithful wife, Capitu is more a victim than an ideological champion. Her identity as a rebel for an ideological cause depends at least to some extent on her being an adulteress because we tend to see her adultery as an act of self-assertion and a breaking away from patriarchal bondage. Ironically, we cannot acknowledge this more radical ideology unless as readers we repudiate the same ideology, going along with a patriarchal reading and adhering to the authority of Santiago's account. We may adopt a more radical reading, contrary to Santiago's authority, and find Capitu innocent. But if we do this, the internal ideology of the novel seems much less radical, since Capitu is now a faithful wife and a victim and much less aggressive in opposing Bentinho's domination.

Published on the threshold of this century, *Dom Casmurro* took the theme of adultery, one of the favorites of the realistic novel of the nineteenth century, and imbued it with a veritable cosmos of questions that would become central concerns of the twentieth century. Many of these questions gravitate around the matter of essences. Is there or is there not something essential in human beings or in their relationships with each other and the universe? The novel asks related questions about literature: Is or is not textual meaning determinate? If it tells us anything, *Dom Casmurro* seems to tell us that at least in present circumstances these questions have no clear answers.

As I pointed out in chapter 6, Bentinho and Capitu are closest when they acknowledge their condition of scarcity. Once their needs in various areas are satisfied, their marriage begins to have problems. Solutions, particularly Bentinho's ultimate "solution" of the enigma of Capitu, ironically bring about dissolution. This circumstance would seem to imply that the marriage might have survived had the scarcity somehow remained. The implication applies to other levels of meaning in the work.

Dom Casmurro is about many shortages, but one of the most important is the shortage of knowledge. Lack of knowledge, acknowledged as such, motivates questions and adventurous quests. It is often an antidote to false security and dogmatism and tends to promote compromise. Conviction of possessing knowledge often fosters domination, closed-mindedness, and arrogance.

A landmark of literary ambiguity, *Dom Casmurro* might seem to avoid all assertions. I believe, however, that a positive message is implied in the story the novel did not tell about the marriage of compromise that did not take place. It seems to tell us that judgments are best when made on a very provisional basis. In a sense, asking the questions *is* the answer.

▼

NOTES

Introduction

1. For a more detailed synopsis of Machado's life and works, see Helen Caldwell, *Machado de Assis: The Brazilian Master and His Novels* (Berkeley and Los Angeles: University of California Press, 1970) or Renard Pérez, "Esboço biográfico," in Machado de Assis, *Obra completa*, vol. 1, ed. Afrânio Coutinho (Rio de Janeiro: Nova Aguilar, 1985), 67–92.

2. R. Magalhães Jr., *Vida e obra de Machado de Assis*, vol. 4 (Rio de Janeiro: Civilização Brasileira, 1981), 104.

3. Frank Kermode, *The Sense of an Ending: Studies in the Theory of Fiction* (New York: Oxford University Press, 1967), 97.

4. Tony Tanner, *Adultery in the Novel: Contract and Transgression* (Baltimore, Md.: Johns Hopkins University Press, 1979), 11–12.

5. Tanner, 12. The novels are *La nouvelle Héloïse* (Rousseau); *Die Wahlverwandtschaften* (Goethe); *Madame Bovary* (Flaubert); *Anna Karenina* (Tolstoy); *Effi Briest* and *Unwiederbringlich* (Fontane); *Le rouge et le noir* (Stendahl); *La femme de trente ans, La muse du département, Gobseck*, and *La Duchesse de Langeais* (Balzac); *The Scarlet Letter* (Hawthorne); *The Awakening* (Chopin); *The Age of Innocence* (Wharton); *One of Our Conquerers* (Meredith); *Orley Farm* (Trollope); *Jude the Obscure* (Hardy); *The Good Soldier* (Ford); and *Lady Chatterley's Lover* (Lawrence); plus the two by Machado.

6. Quoted in Irving Howe, *The Idea of the Modern in Literature and the Arts* (New York: Horizon, 1967), 18.

7. Carlos Fuentes, *La nueva narrativa hispanoamericana* (Mexico City: Joaquín Mortiz, 1969), 13.

8. See John Gledson, *The Deceptive Realism of Machado de Assis: A Dissenting Interpretation of* Dom Casmurro (Liverpool: Liverpool Monographs in Hispanic Studies, 1984).

9. See, for example, João Pacheco, *O realismo*, vol. 3 of *A literatura brasileira* (Rio de Janeiro: Cultrix, 1965), 60–64; Dieter Woll, *Machado de Assis* (Braunschweig: Westermann, 1972), 34–42; and Parke Renshaw, "O humor em *Iaiá Garcia e Brás Cubas*," *Luso-Brazilian Review* 9 (1972): 13–20.

10. Fuentes, 24–27.

11. Fuentes, 11.

12. Fuentes, 12.

13. Fuentes, 14.

14. Fuentes, 25.

15. Fuentes, 30.

16. Fuentes, 24.

17. Kermode, 104.

18. Kermode, 105.

19. Kermode, 104.

20. Kermode, 113.

21. See Maria Luisa Nunes, *The Craft of an Absolute Winner: Characterization and Narratology in the Novels of Machado de Assis* (Westport, Conn.: Greenwood Press, 1983), 64–87. The concept of the "implied author" is from Wayne Booth, *The Rhetoric of Fiction* (Chicago: University of Chicago Press, 1961).

Chapter One

1. Machado de Assis, *Dom Casmurro*, in vol. 1 of *Obra completa*, ed. Afrânio Coutinho (Rio de Janeiro: Nova Aguilar, 1985). Translations of the passages are from Helen Caldwell's translation, *Dom Casmurro* (Berkeley and Los Angeles: University of California Press, 1966). No translation can perfectly capture the nuances or structure of the original language. Consequently, the exact wording of Caldwell's very good translation occasionally seems anomalous in light of certain points I want to make. In these rare cases (chapters 3, 32, 37, 64, 132, 134, and 148) I have taken the liberty of amending. Except where otherwise noted, translations of citations from all other sources are my own.

2. Massaud Moisés, "Machado de Assis e o realismo," *Anhembi* 35, No. 105 (1959): 469–79.

3. Moisés, 476.

4. For convincing support of the idea that Machado included realistic geographic detail in his works, see Waldir Ribeiro do Val, *Geografia*

de Machado de Assis (Rio de Janeiro: São José, 1977). In *The City in Brazilian Literature* (Rutherford, N.J.: Fairleigh Dickinson University Press, 1982), Elizabeth Lowe concludes that "Assis's rendering of the city stands as a peak of literary achievement, not only in the evolution of nineteenth-century urban fiction, but in the entire course of Brazilian city writing" (88–89).

5. Moisés, 476. For similar opinions on the absence of local color, see Moysés Vellinho, *Machado de Assis: histórias mal contadas e outros assuntos* (Rio de Janeiro: São José, 1960), 13–34; and Agrippino Grieco, *Viagem em torno a Machado de Assis* (São Paulo: Martins, n.d.), 76–78. A recent and at times quite convincing argument for *Dom Casmurro* as *exterior* realism primarily concerned with contemporary politics is John Gledson, *The Deceptive Realism of Machado de Assis: A Dissenting Interpretation of* Dom Casmurro (Liverpool: Liverpool Monographs in Hispanic Studies, 1984).

6. Moisés, 476.

7. Charles Baudelaire, "Le peintre de la vie moderne," In *Œuvres Complètes* (Paris: Gallimard, 1961), 1163.

8. See Eugênio Gomes, "O testamento estético de Machado de Assis," in *Machado de Assis* (Rio de Janeiro: São José, 1958), 175–215, a kind of catalog of mythic motifs in *Esaú e Jacó;* Winifred H. Osta and Michael Fody, III, "The Anima Figure in the Later Novels of Machado de Assis," *Kentucky Romance Quarterly* 26 (1978): 67–79, an overview with some discussion of *Dom Casmurro;* Affonso Romano de Sant'Anna, *Análise estrutural de romances brasileiros* (Petrópolis: Vozes, 1973), 116–52, a discussion of the "suporte mítico" of *Esaú e Jacó;* and Donaldo Schüler, *Plenitude perdida: uma análise das seqüências narrativas no romance* Dom Casmurro *de Machado de Assis* (Porto Alegre: Movimento, 1978), a structural analysis according to the theory of Vladimir Propp and the most complete treatment to date of mythic elements in the novel.

9. Bernice Slote, ed. introduction to Northrop Frye et al., *Myth and Symbol: Critical Approaches and Applications* (Lincoln: University of Nebraska Press, 1963), v.

10. Northrop Frye, *Anatomy of Criticism: Four Essays* (Princeton, N.J.:   Princeton University Press, 1957), 136–38.

11. See, for example, Eric Gould, *Mythical Intentions in Modern Literature* (Princeton, N.J.: Princeton University Press, 1981), 15–31; Robert E. Scholes, *Structuralism in Literature: An Introduction* (New Haven, Conn.: Yale University Press, 1974), 118–27; Tzvetan Todorov, *Introduction à la littérature fantastique*

(Paris: Seuil, 1970), 13–27; and K. K. Ruthven, *Myth* (London: Methuen, 1976), 19–21.

12. See Ruthven's criticism of this tendency, 80–81.

13. See Daphne Patai, *Myth and Ideology in Contemporary Brazilian Fiction* (Rutherford, N.J.: Fairleigh Dickinson University Press, 1983), 76.

14. See Juan Villegas, *La estructura mítica del héroe en la novela del siglo XX* (Barcelona: Planeta, 1973), 29–30.

15. See, for example, Elizabeth Closs Traugott and Mary Louise Pratt, *Linguistics for Students of Literature* (New York: Harcourt, Brace, Jovanovich, 1980), 24–29.

16. For general notions on generative grammar, see Traugott and Pratt, 12–19; and Noam Chomsky, *Language and Mind*, enl. ed. (New York: Harcourt, Brace, Jovanovich, 1972), 24–64.

17. Susanna Egan, *Patterns of Experience in Autobiography* (Chapel Hill: University of North Carolina Press, 1984), 14.

18. Paul John Eakin, *Fictions in Autobiography: Studies in the Art of Self-Invention* (Princeton, N.J.: Princeton University Press, 1985), 3.

19. Enylton de Sá Rego, "The Epic, the Comic and the Tragic: Tradition and Innovation in Three Late Novels of Machado de Assis," *Latin American Literary Review* 14:27 (1986): 19–34.

20. Helen Caldwell, *Machado de Assis: The Brazilian Master and His Novels* (Berkeley and Los Angeles: University of California Press, 1970), 102–10.

21. Joseph Campbell, *The Hero with a Thousand Faces* (New York: World, 1956), 30; Northrop Frye, *Fables of Identity: Studies in Poetic Mythology* (New York: Harcourt, Brace & World, 1963), 15–19; and Vladimir Propp, *Morfología del cuento*, trans. Lourdes Ortiz (Madrid: Fundamentos, 1977), 31–74.

22. Campbell, 30.

23. Campbell, 49–246.

24. See Hayden White's discussion of myth, history, the four major tropes, and Frye's four major genres in *Tropics of Discourse: Essays in Cultural Criticism* (Baltimore, Md.: Johns Hopkins University Press, 1978), 51–80.

Chapter Two

1. The most extensive work so far is Dirce Cortes Riedel, *O tempo no romance machadiano* (Rio de Janeiro: São José, 1959). This

contains (197–209) a review of criticism on the subject up to the year of its publication. More recent works are Ione de Andrade, "Machado de Assis e Proust: aproximações," *Estado de São Paulo* (Lit. Suppl.), 2 August 1969, 6; Thiers Martins Moreira, *Visão em vários tempos: 1* (Rio de Janeiro: São José, 1970); Hennio Birchal Morgan, "As personagens e o tempo no *Esaú e Jacó*," *Minas Gerais* (Lit. Suppl.), 28 December 1974, 4–5; Christopher Eustis, "Time and Narrative Structure in *Memórias póstumas de Brás Cubas*," *Luso-Brazilian Review* 16 (1979):18–28; Paula K. Speck, "Narrative Time and the 'Defunto Autor' in *Memórias Póstumas de Brás Cubas*," *Latin American Literary Review* 9 no. 18 (1981):7–15; Maria Luisa Nunes, *The Craft of an Absolute Winner: Characterization and Narratology in the Novels of Machado de Assis* (Westport, Conn.: Greenwood Press, 1983), 88–116, and "Time and Allegory in Machado de Assis' *Esau and Jacob*," *Latin American Literary Review* 11, no. 21 (1982):27–38; Jack Schmitt and Lorie Ishimatsu, translator's introduction to Machado de Assis, *The Devil's Church and Other Stories* (Austin: University of Texas Press, 1977), xii–xiii; David T. Haberley, *Three Sad Races: Racial Identity and National Consciousness in Brazilian Literature* (Cambridge: Cambridge University Press, 1983), 80–86; and Afrânio Coutinho's introduction to Machado's *Obra completa*, vol. 1 (Rio de Janerio: José Aguilar, 1962), 49–51.

2. Riedel, 194.

3. See Tony Tanner, *Adultery in the Novel: Contract and Transgression* (Baltimore, Md.: Johns Hopkins University Press, 1979), 11–24.

4. See Mircea Eliade, *The Myth of the Eternal Return or, Cosmos and History*, trans. Willard R. Trask (Princeton, N.J.:   Princeton University Press, 1954), 34–92; as well as his *The Sacred and the Profane: The Nature of Religion*, trans. Willard R. Trask (Princeton, N.J.:   Princeton University Press, 1964), 68–72, 107. In *Primitive Mentality*, trans. Lilian A. Clare (Boston: Beacon Press, 1966), 93–94, Lucien Lévy-Bruhl also postulates an alinear, nonobjective perception of time as a mode of perception for the primitive mind. For him this appears to be *the* way primitives understand time, while for Eliade primitive minds exist in a tension between linear and alinear time, with a preference for the latter. Franz Boas, in *The Mind of Primitive Man*, rev. ed. (New York: Macmillan, 1938), 226–52, does not discuss primitive man's perception of time *per se,* but suggests his reaction against chronological time by discussing his essential conservatism. He says primitive man is primarily emotional rather than rational and finds emotional stability in custom and tradition. The primitive resists change because of the affective dissonance it brings. According to Boas, the historicism or changeability of modern

civilization is the result of the triumph of reason over the emotions. For a discussion of some ideological implications of the cultivation of origins, see Daphne Patai, *Myth and Ideology in Contemporary Brazilian Fiction* (Rutherford, N.J.: Fairleigh Dickinson University Press, 1983), 64–69.

5. See George Lakoff and Mark Johnson, *Metaphors We Live By* (Chicago: University of Chicago Press, 1980), 3–13, 41–44.

6. Machado de Assis, *Memórias póstumas de Brás Cubas*, in vol. 1 of *Obra completa*, ed. Afrânio Coutinho (Rio de Janeiro: Nova Aguilar, 1985), 519–20.

7. See Susanne K. Langer, *Philosophy in a New Key: A Study in the Symbolism of Reason, Rite and Art* (Cambridge, Mass.:   Harvard University Press, 1942), 144–70.

8. Donaldo Schüler, *Plenitude perdida: uma análise das seqüências narrativas no romance* Dom Casmurro *de Machado de Assis* (Porto Alegre: Movimento, 1978), 17–18. Schüler also associates the house with the cosmos and calls its rebuilding a manifestation of the creation myth.

Chapter Three

1. See Robert E. Ornstein, *On the Experience of Time* (Middlesex: Penguin, 1969), 38.

2. Northrop Frye, *Fables of Identity: Studies in Poetic Mythology* (New York: Harcourt, Brace & World, 1963), 15–17.

3. Maud Bodkin, *Archetypal Patterns in Poetry: Psychological Studies in Imagination* (1934; rpt. London: Oxford University Press, 1965), 89.

4. See Bodkin, 26–60; Joseph Campbell, *The Hero with a Thousand Faces* (New York: World, 1971), 90–94.

5. Donaldo Schüler also discusses the novel's structure as a life/death cycle. See *Plenitude perdida: uma análise das seqüências narrativas no romance* Dom Casmurro *de Machado de Assis* (Porto Alegre: Movimento, 1978), 56–59.

6. See Boris Tomashevsky, "Thematics," in *Russian Formalist Criticism: Four Essays*, trans. and ed. Lee T. Lemon and Marion D. Reis (Lincoln: University of Nebraska Press, 1965), 68.

7. See Bodkin, 47–48.

8. See Northrop Frye, *Anatomy of Criticism: Four Essays* (Princeton, N. J.:   Princeton University Press, 1957), 203–6.

9. Frye, *Anatomy*, 146.

10. See Schüler, 55, 65.

11. See Bodkin, 52.

12. Joaquim-Francisco Coelho identifies this fluctuation, characterizing Bentinho as a person with "um temperamento tímido e indeciso, oscilando entre o pensar e o agir, entre a vontade de poder e a impotência da vontade," and analyzes a specific example of this behavior in "Um processo metafórico de *Dom Casmurro*," *Revista Iberoamericana* 36 (1970):465–72.

Chapter Four

1. Machado de Assis, "Advertência da primeira edição," in *Ressurreição*, vol. 1 of *Obras completas* (Rio de Janeiro: Jackson, 1962), 9. The orthography in this and other citations from the Jackson editions has been modernized.

2. Machado de Assis, "Advertência de 1874," in *A Mão e a luva*, vol. 2 of *Obras completas* (Rio de Janeiro: Jackson, 1962), n.p.

3. Machado de Assis, *Crítica literária*, vol. 29 of *Obras completas* (Rio de Janeiro: Jackson, 1962), 160.

4. Machado de Assis, *Crítica,* 159.

5. Machado de Assis, *Crítica*, 162–63.

6. Machado de Assis, *Crítica*, 163.

7. Machado de Assis, *Crítica*, 171.

8. The theme of jealousy has been studied from various angles. See Charles Param, "Jealousy in the Novels of Machado de Assis," *Hispania* 53 (1970):198–206, for an overview of several studies. Critics have tended to concentrate on the effects of jealousy, for example, Bentinho's jealousy makes him unreliable as a narrator, or have simply mentioned jealousy as a point of comparison between works. Param explores the causes of jealousy but looks into the author's biography rather than into the works themselves for these causes. Here we propose to place jealousy within a broad perspective by considering it as one of several effects of an underlying value system within the novel.

9. See, for example, J. J. Bachofen, *Myth, Religion, and Mother Right*, trans. Ralph Manheim (Princeton, N.J.: Princeton University Press, 1967), 69–120; Bronislaw Malinowski, *The Father in Primitive Psychology* (London: Basic English, n.d.), all 93 pp.; Erich Neumann, "The Moon and Matriarchal Consciousness," in

Augusto Vitale et al., *Fathers and Mothers: Five Papers on the Archetypal Background of Family Psychology* (Zurich: Spring Publications, 1973), 40–63; and Erich Fromm, *The Forgotten Language: An Introduction to the Understanding of Dreams, Fairy Tales and Myths* (New York: Rinehart, 1951), 204–9. The approaches used by these four writers are complementary. Bachofen attempts to prove the historicity of a matriarchal society before the rise of patriarchal ones. According to Franz Boas (see preface, xi), that theory has been almost universally discredited. But Joseph Campbell (introduction, xxv–xxviii) says his findings remain valid for what they reveal about the profound psychological laws at the basis of mythology. Malinowski's work is a case study of a matrilineal society in the Trobriand Islands near New Guinea. Discussion of patriarchy is introduced by way of contrast. Neumann's is a psychological discussion, concentrating on perceptual biases of both systems. Fromm's approach is closest to that of this study in that it uses the concepts of patriarchy and matriarchy as a theoretical construct for analyzing myths and literature.

10. For discussion of matriarchal and patriarchal conceptions of the hero, see Carol Pearson and Katherine Pope, *The Female Hero in American and British Literature* (New York: Bowker, 1981), 3–15; and Annis Pratt, *Archetypal Patterns in Women's Fiction* (Bloomington: Indiana University Press, 1981), 167–78.

11. See also Sylvio Rabello, *Caminhos da província* (Recife: Imprensa Universitária da Universidade do Recife, 1965), 15–23. Rabello correctly affirms that Capitu places a high value upon maternity. He identifies Bentinho's position as one of traditional bourgeois values and notes the values' "resíduos patriarcais" (patriarchal residues). By implication, he attributes many of the matriarchal values to Capitu but by and large concentrates upon her rather vaguely defined "feminilidade" (femininity), which he says is fighting to cast off the shackles of male domination and eventually triumphs, with "a vitória da mulher sobre o homem, da feminilidade sobre a masculinidade" (the victory of woman over man, of femininity over masculinity). Rabello's "victory" is based upon the assumption that Capitu deliberately betrayed her husband in order to fulfill her maternal instincts: "Ela acabou traindo este homem. Mas de nenhum modo ela traiu a si mesma— à sua feminilidade gloriosamente feita para a fecundação" (She ended up betraying this man. But in no way did she betray herself—her femininity, gloriously created for procreation). However, if the equally plausible hypothesis is true that Capitu remained faithful to Bentinho and was but the victim of his excessive jealousy, there seems to be less of a case for a victory. As

this study will attempt to show, both parties in a sense achieve a "victory" by adhering at all costs to their principles, but the victory for both sides has extremely high costs and might even be considered a mutual defeat.

John Gledson, *The Deceptive Realism of Machado de Assis: A Dissenting Interpretation of* Dom Casmurro (Liverpool: Liverpool Monographs in Hispanic Studies, 1984), concurs that "the patriarchal norm [in Bentinho's family] remains in operation, even when the father is dead: indeed, when he is dead, its results are yet more destructive than if he were alive" (60).

12. See Keith Ellis, "Technique and Ambiguity in '*Dom Casmurro*,' " *Hispania* 45 (1962):436–40.

13. Neumann, 41–45.

14. For example, Bentinho says he envies Escobar's strong arms. On this occasion, Escobar invites him to go swimming, saying, "O mar amanhã está de desafiar a gente" (The sea tomorrow will be a challenge—chap. 118), but Bentinho declines.

15. Bentinho is not satisfied until according to his perception he receives such a confession. He says he was almost to conclude he was the victim of a "grande ilusão" when Ezequiel runs into the room. Both he and Capitu look involuntarily at Escobar's portrait on the wall. He concludes, "A confusão dela fez-se confissão pura" (Her confusion amounted to pure confession—chap. 139).

16. Helen Caldwell points out this etymologic dimension in the name but sees it as a reference to Bentinho's "belief in a special relationship with God," rather than as a mark of a general domineering nature. See *Machado de Assis: The Brazilian Master and His Novels* (Berkeley and Los Angeles: University of California Press, 1970), 145–46.

17. See, for example, an "authoritarian" viewpoint in E. D. Hirsch, Jr., *Validity in Interpretation* (New Haven, Conn.:   Yale University Press, 1967), 1–23; and a contrary viewpoint in Jonathan Culler, *Structuralist Poetics: Structuralism, Linguistics and the Study of Literature* (Ithaca, N.Y.:   Cornell University Press, 1975), 116–18, 241–54.

Chapter Five

1. See Northrop Frye, *Anatomy of Criticism: Four Essays* (Princeton, N.J.:   Princeton University Press, 1957), 33–34.

2. C. G. Jung, "Archetypes of the Collective Unconscious," in *The Collected Works of C. G. Jung,* vol. 9, part 1, trans. R. F. C. Hull, ed. Herbert Read et al. (New York: Pantheon, 1959), 24–25.

3. See Eugênio Gomes, *O enigma de Capitu: ensaio de interpretação* (Rio de Janeiro: José Olympio, 1967), 102; Winifred Osta and Michael Fody, III, "The 'Anima Figure' in the Later Novels of Machado de Assis," *Kentucky Romance Quarterly* 26 (1979):73–75; and Donaldo Schüler, *Plenitude perdida: uma análise das seqüências narrativas no romance* Dom Casmurro *de Machado de Assis* (Porto Alegre: Movimento, 1978), 52.

4. According to Linhares Filho, this sexual dimension is *the* underlying meaning of the metaphor and the novel. See *A metáfora do mar no* Dom Casmurro (Rio de Janeiro: Tempo Brasileiro, 1978), 61–83. I accept his findings but not to the exclusion of other levels of meaning as he seems to advocate.

5. C. G. Jung, "Concerning the Archetypes, with Special Reference to the Anima Concept," in *The collected Works of C. G. Jung,* vol. 9, part 1, trans. R. F. C. Hull, ed. Herbert Read et al. (New York: Pantheon, 1959), 71–72.

6. See Joseph Campbell, *The Hero with a Thousand Faces* (New York: World, 1956), 120–26, 246.

7. See Paul B. Dixon, *Reversible Readings: Ambiguity in Four Modern Latin American Novels* (University: University of Alabama Press, 1985), 51–52, for mention of several metonymies connecting Capitu with writing.

8. See Jonathan Culler, *Structuralist Poetics: Structuralism, Linguistics and the Study of Literature* (Ithaca, N.Y.:   Cornell University Press, 1975), 139–40.

9. This is one of the main ideas of Helen Caldwell, *The Brazilian Othello of Machado de Assis: A Study of* Dom Casmurro (Berkeley and Los Angeles: University of California Press, 1960).

10. Schüler, 52, points out Machado's allusion to Camões' Thetis and discusses the tradition of alluring and destroying sea goddesses. He also calls the scene of "A denúncia" (chap. 3), in which D. Glória and other members of the household discuss Bentinho's future, a kind of "concílio dos deuses." This council is an important part of the *Odyssey,* the *Iliad,* and of course, *Os Lusíadas.*

11. Spelling in earlier editions confirms that the novel refers to Adamastor's Thetis, and not Tethys, wife of Ocean, who had three thousand children. In modern Portuguese both names are spelled the same. See also Massaud Moisés, note on 223 to Machado de Assis, *Dom Casmurro,* 2nd ed. (São Paulo: Cultrix, n. d.)

12. Luís de Camões, *Os Lusíadas,* ed. Frank Pierce (Oxford: Oxford University Press, 1973), 122.

13. See Schüler, 62:   "Com a reflexão de Marcolini, o conflito partic-
    ular da narrative adquire dimensões universais. Na autobiografia
    reflete-se a história."

14. For a review of criticism on the novel's ambiguity, see Dixon,
    28–29, 161–62.

Chapter Six

1. See Northrop Frye, *Anatomy of Criticism: Four Essays* (Princeton, N.J.:   Princeton University Press, 1957), 186–95.

2. James George Frazer, *The Golden Bough: A Study in Magic and
   Religion,* abridged ed. (New York: Macmillan, 1951), 12–14,
   43–55.

3. Frazer, 12, 12–43.

4. See Henrique Howens Post, "El autor brasileño. Machado de
   Assis y el mito de Sísifo," trans. Pilar Gómez Bedate, *Revista de
   cultura brasileña 1,* no. 3 (1962):185–95.

5. See A. H. Quiggin, *The Story of Money* (London: Methuen,
   1958), 1.

6. John Kenneth Galbraith, *Money, Whence it Came, Where it Went*
   (Boston: Houghton Mifflin, 1975), 5.

7. Linhares Filho discusses the sexual suggestiveness of money in *A
   metáfora do mar no* Dom Casmurro (Rio de Janeiro: Tempo
   Brasileiro, 1978), 92–122.

8. For an interesting discussion of the underlying aggressiveness of
   gift-giving, see Marcel Mauss, *The Gift: Forms and Functions of
   Exchange in Archaic Societies,* trans. Ian Cunnison (Glencoe, Ill.:
   Free Press, 1954), especially 62.

9. See Walter J. Ong, *Orality and Literacy: The Technologies of the
   Word* (London: Methuen, 1982), 29; Jack Goody, *The Domestica-
   tion of the Savage Mind* (Cambridge: Cambridge University
   Press, 1977), 146–51; and Marshall McLuhan, *The Gutenberg
   Galaxy: The Making of Typographic Man* (Toronto: University
   of Toronto Press, 1962), 20–23.

10. See Quiggin, 2–5.

Epilogue

1. See Kenneth Burke, *A Grammar of Motives* (New York: Prentice-
   Hall, 1945), 503–17.

2. See Paul B. Dixon, *Reversible Readings: Ambiguity in Four Modern Latin American Novels* (University: University of Alabama Press, 1985), 52–55.

3. See Daphne Patai, *Myth and Ideology in Contemporary Brazilian Fiction* (Rutherford, N.J.: Fairleigh Dickinson University Press, 1983), 76.

4. See Helen Caldwell, *The Brazilian Othello of Machado de Assis: A Study of* Dom Casmurro (Berkeley and Los Angeles: University of California Press, 1960), 2.

Andrade, Ione de. "Machado de Assis e Proust: aproximações." *Estado de São Paulo* (Lit. Suppl.), 2 August 1969, p. 6.

Assis, Machado de. "Advertência da primeria edição." In *Ressurreição.* Vol. 1 of *Obras completas.* Rio de Janeiro: Jackson, 1962.

_____ . "Advertência de 1874." In *A mão e a luva.* Vol. 2 of *Obras completas.* Rio de Janeiro: Jackson, 1962.

_____ . *Crítica literária.* Vol. 29 of *Obras completas.* Rio de Janeiro: Jackson, 1962.

_____ . *The Devil's Church and Other Stories.* Trans. Jack Schmitt and Lorie Ishimatsu. Austin: University of Texas Press, 1977.

_____ . *Dom Casmurro.* 2nd ed. Ed. Massaud Moisés. São Paulo: Cultrix, n. d.

_____ . *Dom Casmurro.* Trans. Helen Caldwell. Berkeley and Los Angeles: University of California Press, 1966.

_____ . *Obra completa.* Vol. 1. Ed. Afrânio Coutinho. Rio de Janeiro: Nova Aguilar, 1985.

Bachofen, J. J. *Myth, Religion, and Mother Right.* Trans. Ralph Manheim. Princeton, N.J.: Princeton University Press, 1967.

Baudelaire, Charles. "Le peintre de la vie moderne." In *Œuvres complètes,* 1158-68. Paris: Gallimard, 1961.

Boas, Franz. *The Mind of Primitive Man.* Rev. ed. New York: Macmillan, 1938.

Bodkin, Maud. *Archetypal Patterns in Poetry: Psychological Studies in Imagination.* 1934; rpt. London: Oxford University Press, 1965.

Booth, Wayne. *The Rhetoric of Fiction.* Chicago: University of Chicago Press, 1961.

Burke, Kenneth. *A Grammar of Motives.* New York: Prentice-Hall, 1945.

Caldwell, Helen. *The Brazilian Othello of Machado de Assis: A Study of* Dom Casmurro. Berkeley and Los Angeles: University of California Press, 1960.

_____ . *Machado de Assis: The Brazilian Master and His Novels.* Berkeley and Los Angeles: University of California Press, 1970.

Camões, Luís de. *Os Lusíadas.* Ed. Frank Pierce. Oxford: Oxford University Press, 1973.

Campbell, Joseph. *The Hero with a Thousand Faces.* New York: World, 1956.

Chomsky, Noam. *Language and Mind.* Enl. ed. New York: Harcourt, Brace and Jovanovich, 1972.

Coelho, Joaquim-Francisco. "Um processo metafórico de *Dom Casmurro.*" *Revista Iberoamericana* 36 (1970):465–72.

Culler, Jonathan. *Structuralist Poetics: Structuralism, Linguistics and the Study of Literature.* Ithaca, N.Y.: Cornell University Press, 1975.

Dixon, Paul B. *Reversible Readings: Ambiguity in Four Modern Latin American Novels.* University: University of Alabama Press, 1985.

Eakin, Paul John. *Fictions in Autobiography: Studies in the Art of Self-Invention.* Princeton, N.J.: Princeton University Press, 1985.

Egan, Susanna. *Patterns of Experience in Autobiography.* Chapel Hill: University of North Carolina Press, 1984.

Eliade, Mircea. *The Myth of the Eternal Return or, Cosmos and History.* Trans. Willard R. Trask. Princeton, N.J.: Princeton University Press, 1954.

_____ . *The Sacred and the Profane: The Nature of Religion.* Trans. Willard R. Trask. Princeton, N.J.: Princeton University Press, 1964.

Ellis, Keith. "Technique and Ambiguity in 'Dom Casmurro.'" *Hispania* 45 (1965):436–40.

Eustis, Christopher. "Time and Narrative Structure in *Memórias póstumas de Brás Cubas.*" *Luso-Brazilian Review* 16 (1979): 18–28.

Frazer, James George. *The Golden Bough: A Study In Magic and Religion.* Abridged ed. New York: Macmillan, 1951.

Fromm, Erich. *The Forgotten Language: An Introduction to the Understanding of Dreams, Fairy Tales and Myths.* New York: Rinehart, 1951.

Frye, Northrop. *Anatomy of Criticism: Four Essays*. Princeton, N.J.: Princeton University Press, 1957.

_____ . *Fables of Identity: Studies in Poetic Mythology*. New York: Harcourt, Brace and World, 1963.

_____ , et al. *Myth and Symbol: Critical Approaches and Applications*. Lincoln: University of Nebraska Press, 1963.

Fuentes, Carlos. *La nueva narrativa hispanoamericana*. Mexico City: Joaquín Mortiz, 1969.

Galbraith, John Kenneth. *Money, Whence it Came, Where it Went*. Boston: Houghton Mifflin, 1975.

Gledson, John. *The Deceptive Realism of Machado de Assis: A Dissenting Interpretation of* Dom Casmurro. Liverpool: Liverpool Monographs in Hispanic Studies, 1984.

Gomes, Eugênio. *O enigma de Capitu: ensaio de interpretação*. Rio de Janeiro: José Olympio, 1967.

_____ . *Machado de Assis*. Rio de Janeiro: São José, 1958.

Goody, Jack. *The Domestication of The Savage Mind*. Cambridge: Cambridge University Press, 1977.

Gould, Eric. *Mythical Intentions in Modern Literature*. Princeton, N.J.: Princeton University Press, 1981.

Grieco, Agrippino. *Viagem em torno a Machado de Assis*. São Paulo: Martins, n.d.

Haberley, David T. *Three Sad Races: Racial Identity and National Consciousness in Brazilian Literature*. Cambridge: Cambridge University Press, 1985.

Hirsch, E. D., Jr. *Validity in Interpretation*. New Haven, Conn.: Yale University Press, 1967.

Howe, Irving. *The Idea of the Modern in Literature and the Arts*. New York: Horizon, 1967.

Jung, C. G. "Archetypes of the Collective Unconscious." In *The Collected Works of C. G. Jung*. Vol. 9, part 1. Trans. R. F. C. Hull. Ed. Herbert Read et al., 3–41. New York: Pantheon, 1959.

_____ . "Concerning the Archetypes, with Special Reference to the Anima Concept." In *The Collected Works of C. G. Jung*. Vol. 9, part 1. Trans. R. F. C. Hull. Ed. Herbert Read et al., 54–74. New York: Pantheon, 1959.

Kermode, Frank. *The Sense of an Ending: Studies in the Theory of Fiction*. New York: Oxford University Press, 1967.

Lakoff, George, and Mark Johnson. *Metaphors We Live By*. Chicago: University of Chicago Press, 1980.

Langer, Susanne K. *Philosophy in a New Key: A Study in the Symbolism of Reason, Rite and Art*. Cambridge, Mass.: Harvard University Press, 1942.

Lévy-Bruhl, Lucien. *Primitive Mentality*. Trans. Lilian A. Clare. Boston: Beacon, 1966.

Linhares Filho. *A metáfora do mar no* Dom Casmurro. Rio de Janeiro: Tempo Brasileiro, 1978.

Lowe, Elizabeth. *The City in Brazilian Literature*. Rutherford, N.J.: Fairleigh Dickinson University Press, 1982.

Magalhães Jr., R. *Vida e obra de Machado de Assis*. 4 vols. Rio de Janeiro: Civilização Brasileira, 1981.

Malinowski, Bronislaw. *The Father in Primitive Psychology*. London: Basic English, n.d.

Mauss, Marcel. *The Gift: Forms and Functions of Exchange in Archaic Societies*. Trans. Ian Cunnison. Glencoe, Ill.: Free Press, 1954.

McLuhan, Marshall. *The Gutenberg Galaxy: The Making of Typographic Man*. Toronto: University of Toronto Press, 1962.

Moisés, Massaud. "Machado de Assis e o realismo." *Anhembi* 35, no. 105 (1959):469–79.

Moreira, Thiers Martins. *Visão em Vários tempos:* 1. Rio de Janeiro: São José, 1970.

Morgan, Hennio Birchal. "As personagens e o tempo no *Esaú e Jacó*." *Minas Gerais* (Lit. Suppl.), 28 December 1974, 4–5.

Neumann, Eric. "The Moon and Matriarchal Consciousness." In Augusto Vitale et al. *Fathers and Mothers: Five Papers on the Archetypal Background of Family Psychology*, 40–63. Zurich: Spring Publications, 1973.

Nunes, Maria Luisa. *The Craft of an Absolute Winner: Characterization and Narratology in the Novels of Machado de Assis*. Westport, Conn.: Greenwood Press, 1983.

————. "Time and Allegory in Machado de Assis' *Esau and Jacob*." *Latin American Literary Review* 11, no. 21 (1982):27–38.

Ong, Walter J. *Orality and Literacy: The Technologies of the Word*. London: Methuen, 1982.

Ornstein, Robert E. *On the Experience of Time*. Middlesex: Penguin, 1969.

Osta, Winifred H., and Michael Fody, III. "The Anima Figure in the Later Novels of Machado de Assis." *Kentucky Romance Quarterly* 26 (1978):67–79.

Pacheco, João. *O realismo*. Vol. 3 of *A literatura brasileira*. Rio de Janeiro: Cultrix, 1965.

Param, Charles. "Jealousy in the Novels of Machado de Assis." *Hispania* 53 (1970):198–206.

Patai, Daphne. *Myth and Ideology in Contemporary Brazilian Fiction*. Rutherford, N.J.: Fairleigh Dickinson University Press, 1983.

Pearson, Carol, and Katherine Pope. *The Female Hero in American and British Literature*. New York: Bowker, 1981.

Post, Henrique Howens. "El autor brasileño. Machado de Assis y el mito de Sísifo." Trans. Pilar Gómez Bedate. *Revista de Cultura Brasileña* 1, no. 3 (1962):185–95.

Pratt, Annis, *Archetypal Patterns in Women's Fiction*. Bloomington: Indiana University Press, 1981.

Propp, Vladimir. *Morfología del cuento*. Trans. Lourdes Ortiz. Madrid: Fundamentos, 1977.

Quiggin, A. H. *The Story of Money*. London: Methuen, 1958.

Rabello, Sylvio. *Caminhos da província*. Recife: Imprensa Universitária da Universidade de Recife, 1965.

Rego, Enylton de Sá. "The Epic, the Comic and the Tragic: Tradition and Innovation in Three Late Novels of Machado de Assis." *Latin American Literary Review* 14, no. 27 (1986):19–34.

Renshaw, Park. "O humor em *Iaiá Garcia* e *Brás Cubas*." *Luso-Brazilian Review* 9 (1972):13–20.

Riedel, Dirce Cortes. *O tempo no romance machadiano*. Rio de Janeiro: São José, 1959.

Ruthven, K. K. *Myth*. London: Methuen, 1976.

Sant'Anna, Affonso Romano de. *Análise estrutural de romances brasileiros*. Petrópolis: Vozes, 1973.

Scholes, Robert E. *Structuralism in Literature: An Introduction*. New Haven, Conn.: Yale University Press, 1974.

Schüler, Donaldo. *Plenitude perdida: uma análise das seqüências narrativas no romance* Dom Casmurro *de Machado de Assis*. Porto Alegre: Movimento, 1978.

Speck, Paula K. "Narrative Time and The 'Defunto Autor' in *Memórias póstumas de Brás Cubas*." *Latin American Literary Review* 9, no. 18 (1981):7–15.

Tanner, Tony. *Adultery in the Novel: Contract and Transgression.* Baltimore, Md.: Johns Hopkins University Press, 1979.

Todorov, Tzvetan. *Introduction à la littérature fantastique.* Paris: Seuil, 1970.

Tomashevsky, Boris. "Thematics." In Lee T. Lemon and Marion D. Reis, trans. and ed. *Russian Formalist Criticism: Four Essays,* 61–95. Lincoln: University of Nebraska Press, 1965.

Traugott, Elizabeth Cross, and Mary Louise Pratt. *Linguistics for Students of Literature.* New York: Harcourt, Brace Jovanovich, 1980.

Val, Waldir Ribeiro do. *Geografia de Machado de Assis.* Rio de Janeiro: São José, 1977.

Vellinho, Moysés. *Machado de Assis: histórias mal contadas e outros assuntos.* Rio de Janeiro: São José, 1960.

Villegas, Juan. *La estructura mítica del héroe en la novela del siglo XX.* Barcelona: Planeta, 1973.

White, Hayden. *Tropics of Discourse: Essays in Cultural Criticism.* Baltimore, Md.: Johns Hopkins University Press, 1978.

Woll, Dieter. *Machado de Assis.* Braunschweig: Westermann, 1972.